Tramp

Tramp

OR THE ART OF LIVING A WILD AND POETIC LIFE

TOMAS ESPEDAL

TRANSLATED BY JAMES ANDERSON

Seagull
BOOKS

LONDON NEW YORK CALCUTTA

Seagull Books, 2022

Originally published in Norwegian as *GÅ. Eller kunsten å leve et vilt og poetisk liv* by Tomas Espedal

© Gyldendal Norsk Forlag AS 2006. All rights reserved.

First published in English translation by Seagull Books, 2010
English translation © James Anderson 2009

This translation has been published with the financial support of NORLA

ISBN 978 1 80309 030 6

British Library Cataloguing-in-Publication Data
A catalogue record for this book is available
from the British Library

Typeset by Seagull Books, Calcutta, India
Printed and bound in the USA by Versa Press, Ill.

To my father

PART 1

Why not begin with a street

Why not begin with a street. The street and the route I walked, up and down, almost every day for more than two years. Bjørnsonsgate, dirty and car-choked, working class housing in rows on each side of the shadow that resembles a road, a traffic artery, bloodless and cold, a narrow pavement past factory lots, the filling station, down towards Danmarksplass, the city's darkest traffic light intersection. A miserable street, punctuated with depressing relics: a dying tree, that ruinous wooden house and a hedge smothered with exhaust dust, the window where she stands pulling off her cotton jumper.

A miserable street, my home and favourite route into the city. (Today—living on the other side of town, in a bright, clean flat with a terrace and a view of the harbour—I sometimes get the bus to Bjørnsonsgate just to walk down the street, take the old route into the city.) The street opens on to the Technical College and the Krohnsminde Stadium on the right, the high-rise blocks and Solheimsviken on the left, I pass the trainee chefs on the stone steps of the college, they stand smoking under their white, airy cooks' hats, as if they're balancing the clouds on their heads, seven or eight trainee chefs next to the trainee hairdressers, easy to spot because of their hairstyles, red and green shocks of hair of every size and shape (one of the girls has shaved a bare stripe from her forehead to the nape of her neck, it looks as if the street runs straight through her head) and I carry on, down towards Danmarksplass. Down under the traffic tumult. Right or the left through the underpass? The tunnel divides, today I take the right fork and, in retrospect, I should be grateful that I didn't choose the left, because a bit further along on the right, just past the Forum Cinema, after the slope leading to the lake, on the bridge where fish lie dying on the tarmac, the sunlight strikes a traffic sign and I am struck by an unexpected shaft of happiness. It simply says: you are happy. Here and now. For no reason. In this instant you are happy, unreasoningly, like a gift. There's no other way to describe it. I have no cause to be happy, hungover and dejected after four days of solid drinking, living on my own in a filthy house in a miserable street, sleeping on a mattress, without furniture, deserted by the woman I thought I'd be able to live with. I'm in the process of destroying myself, a grim and determined effort at self-destruction, drinking and going to pieces, and suddenly I'm happy. Why? Because sunlight picks out a road sign? I have to stop and catch my breath. I feel a warm and jubilant transparency inside me. Thoughts reawaken and lose their dullness, it's a thoroughly physical experience, my thoughts brighten, and I start walking again, lighter this time, up towards the prominence of Nygårdshøyden and the city centre. Slowly it dawns on me, you're happy because you're walking.

Going to the dogs: crawling, on all fours, belly to the floor, face down, a scar across the eyes, light, it strikes like a cudgel, a wound someone's whistling in, she whistles in my blood, there's a whistling in my head, who is it who's whistling, get closer, crawl across the floor, in under the table, a puddle of alcohol, lap it up, roll over and lie down under the table, you see half or less of everything, a waist, perhaps, naked feet, and in the evenings, the hem of a nightdress. The edge of the table hides the face, it's your father, your lord and master, that beautiful back, the sweat and the shirt, we're moving again. The empty room, so liberatingly empty, a lamp, well, something to love, loving a lamp, getting undressed, switching off the light and going to bed, if only you knew, how can you know, what do you know, he finds the cigarette, crawling under the table, how good it is to crawl, to drown in yourself. How good it is to drink, fill yourself with oblivion, drown.

The falling darkness under the table, like living in a house within a house, Monday, Tuesday, Thursday, a doghouse, you crawl out, roll against the wall, stick the tongue of the belt buckle into the electric socket, there! You see the light, you feel the power, now you can see how he rises, gropes his way to the door, struggles and jerks, jumps for the door handle and reaches it with his mouth, bites it downwards, metal against his tongue, barks open the door and runs out into the corridor, raucous and making all the noises that will make someone come and take him away.

Before I go

Before I go: let's tot up all the joys we know! Drinking, standing, swaying in the bar, lifting the glass, lighting the cigarette, talking without knowing what's being said, a ceaseless stream of oblivion received by any chance mouth.

The next day, crawling, crawling through town, up the stairs, through the door, across the carpet, looking up at the window, playing with the children, talking to them like one demented.

Loving, I mean, pouncing on her, putting on her clothes, panties and tights, vest, jumper, pulling on her hat and coat and seeing her off, and running, at full tilt now, back from nursery school, round the corners and down the stairs, storming into the flat and pouncing on her, pulling off her jumper and tights, panties and vest, getting her into bed, I mean, my life in a nutshell.

Sleeping, a pure pleasure.

Waking, an earnest pleasure, waking each morning, the earnestness of life. It's a joy that life is earnest. You wake, that's a joy, you wake to the earnestness, life wakes, not just you, but your neighbour and the shop, the streets and the noises and the air she no longer breathes.

The joy of life. I love life. The older I get, the more I love life. The more I'm frightened of dying. This surprises me. I'm not getting any wiser with the years, on the contrary, it's almost as if I'm approaching a pure and all-encompassing stupidity.

The joy of staying still, for a long time, of being at home, shut up in the flat, locking the door, turning down the lights, sitting by the lamp and the desk, writing or not writing.

The joy of my desk, of objects, the ashtray and lamp, the window, the chairs, the carpet and the doors. The joy of things. Created by human hands. This house, these stairs, this lift, all the doors and square shapes, books and letters, this desk, this pen, created by language.

It's Tuesday, and today, for the first time, I consider the joy of being able to speak. I rejoice at being able to think, today I rejoice at being able to write, it's Tuesday, and I rejoice that it's Tuesday.

I haven't forgotten the joy of travelling. The thrilling ecstasy of being on the move, sitting in a car and racing along, motionless and at breakneck speed, I love driving fast, fast and far, out of the city, in the darkness, driving at night, out of the city and back again. Or short trips, on bus or boat, out and back the same way; above all I like ferries, or trains, they don't alter their original plans.

We forget. We forget the fundamentals, the joy of waking, of being able to stand up, of going into the kitchen and drinking a glass of water.

A glass of cold water!

I don't know if you can remember . . . the triumph of raising yourself, up from the floor, standing there, swaying, that sudden control and childish joy of being able to walk from room to room.

Walking, that's what I like doing most.

It's Tuesday, and I'm going out. Going out drinking. A foolish joy. The joy of swaying and losing your words and your balance, lurching and crawling, it's almost like being a child again.

An impossible living room

Directly opposite the house on Vestre Torggate, where I lived as a child, is a guest house. Inside the guest house is a bar. Nearly every evening for two years I sat in this bar and drank. From the table I could look up at the window where I'd stood as a child staring down at the lights behind the pane I was sitting next to now.

Sometimes our lives revolve around a few key places and I've found my way back to one of these. A street. It leads upwards, becomes a steep hill and crosses another street before it turns into steps; the steps leading to the church of Johanneskirken. The guest house is on the left, my childhood home on the right; outside the entrance is a square patch of garden and a tree, I think it's a beech, but I'll call it an aspen, inside the front door of the guest house is a horseshoe-shaped bar, and here sits my new family. Yes, the place really does resemble a living room. Here is my drinking brother and my drinking mother and my drinking father, and here is my drinking sister, who gives me beer and cigarettes. But I want to sit alone. I want to drink the first beers alone with the glasses and the counter and the bartender. Look and listen. Hear the same old stories, see the same faces, and be someone else.

Who do you want to be? Who are you meeting? Where will you end up? What will happen? Seating yourself in the bar is like setting out on a journey. Drinking is like travelling without leaving your chair.

'Dark is a way and light is a place', wrote Dylan Thomas. I'm in the light, I've found my customary place in the bar and order a beer. The first one is good. The second is the best. The third is better than the first, the fourth is wonderful, so is the fifth, the rest have nothing to do with taste, but with drinking, with intoxication. A good, gradual oblivion. Not like wine or spirits, nothing so impatient, nothing so excitable; we're going to sit here for a long time, that's the trick, sitting and drinking, a whole evening until night, that's the whole trick: to sit still so long that you're in motion. Travelling slowly and effortlessly away from yourself.

You only need to think the thought: I'll spend an entire life with myself. You can get a new lover, you can leave your family and friends, move away, find new towns and new places, you can sell your possessions and get rid of all the things you don't like but never—as long as you live—can you get rid of yourself.

There are times in life when you say to yourself: I'm an insufferable person. There are times in your life when you want to go to the dogs. Drown. You drink and go to pieces, you sink. You work hard to reach the bottom. You're going down, and the good thing about this work of destruction is that you enjoy it.

There are more straightforward reasons why I drink. I like alcohol. I like this bar. I feel at home here. It's a nice bar. The bar is a good place, a drinking place. The bar is a perverse home, an impossible living room.

It's Tuesday, the best evening. The place is full. I like crowds. To move down into a lower unity, a kind of nether companionship; an intoxicated society. It's just after midnight, it's neither Tuesday nor Wednesday, it's drinking time. It's time to disappear, here amongst your friends and your new family and all the people you don't know. You sit in the bar and drink. You've thrown yourself into the crowd, and without anyone noticing, you sink all the way to the bottom and vanish.

The dream of vanishing

The dream of vanishing. Disappearing. Going out of the door one day and never coming back.

The dream of turning into someone else. Leaving friends and family, leaving your own self and becoming someone else; breaking all ties, going from home and habits, abandoning possessions and security, future plans and ambitions to become a stranger.

Letting your beard grow, your hair lengthen, hiding your eyes, buying a pair of glasses, second-hand clothes, worn-out shoes, your face filling, your hands blackening, moving around in your familiar surroundings, among your old acquaintances, and seeing how it looks when you're gone.

The dream of metamorphosis.

As when you wake up in bed one morning next to a face you don't know. As when you speak your name, and the name seems vacant. As when you get out of bed and can't find the light switch in its usual place, the bedside table has gone, the walls are different, the ceiling lower, and the door, which stands ajar, is on the left of the bed and not on the right as usual. And where is the window? The window overlooking the backyard gives on to a landscape you've never seen before, but which you recognize, perhaps it's from a dream or a previous life, or the landscape belongs to a life you knew would come, a place you knew you would find, now you're there, you stand at the window looking out, and for a moment you're happy: you've forgotten who you are.

Or the dream's doubling, a nightmare: you're standing on the street corner, and there on the other side of the road you see the person you fear more than any other: you see yourself. You can't stop yourself from following him, and you can't help noticing that he's taking a road and a route that you know, one that is your own. He's on his way home, and it's your way and your home. Your name is on his post box. He reads your letters. He seems to know your habits. He's taken your place, that's obvious. What are you going to do? What do you want to do? You want to disappear, but you can be replaced just like that, you've already been replaced, and now, clearly and painfully, you see just how bound up with yourself you really are.

Or the dream's obverse, the dark mirror, you look into the blackness and want to die. How did you get here? You take a step towards the bed or the window; should you throw yourself out into the street, the hard ending, or should you lie down on the bed and swallow a bottle of pills, which do you want? How did you get here? A voice is screaming in your head, another in your ears, a third in your breast, a fourth in your belly: don't do it! But you move towards the window, look down, down at the pavement, the street lights are lit, it's night. You're in your best clothes, your shirt is ironed, your hair combed, your face shaved, as if you're off on a journey, a last journey, how tired I am of travelling, how tired I am of being at home, how tired I am of everything. But, how did I get here, to the window or the bed, to this thought of giving up? I don't want to be found on the pavement, all open and gooey, all exposed and smashed. I choose the bed and go towards it, lie down on it, there's a screaming in my mouth and in my throat, in my hands and in my hand: don't do it!

Or the dream of ceasing to exist, only to rise again as something new, not a beetle, or a flower, or as anything higher or lower, not as nothing, but as in the Christian dream of Lazarus: waking up to a new life. Recognizable to oneself and to others but nevertheless altered. A new person.

It is an old dream. As old as humankind, as the weariness of being. As the dissatisfaction of being yourself. No, I've had enough now. No, I can't take any more. And then this lie, which has slowly turned into an apathy: I've seen it all, heard it all, done it all.

Boredom. Not the good, quiet kind, but suffocating, nauseating, angst-filled boredom. Staring into the great, all-encompassing, empty, meaningless void.

Today I lost my faith. My faith in something new.

All that's left is the repetition of yourself.

What happened to the joys?

The joy of repeating yourself?

Getting up, washing your face, looking at yourself in the mirror, dressing, eating breakfast and sitting down at your desk. Everyday tasks: wearing yourself out trying to find something new, a new word, a new sentence, a new book.

Hast never come to thee an hour,

A sudden gleam divine, precipitating, bursting all these bubbles, fashions, wealth?

These eager business aims—books, politics, art, amours,

To utter nothingness?

So wrote Walt Whitman, and just today, Thursday 19 August at eight forty-three a.m., that hour came to me for the second time. What did I do on the first occasion? I stopped writing. I kept it up for four years. I moved to the country, married and had children, tried life as a crofter but couldn't manage it.

I couldn't manage being married or living in the country, I couldn't manage not to write. I couldn't manage to get rid of myself. I couldn't manage to be another. I missed my former life. I wanted to be alone. Wanted to write books. I shut myself away. I wrote. I resumed my old life again. My old bustle. New relationships. New dreams, new journeys, new fashions, new money, new books. New breakdowns. But never a new life. Do you think it's possible to begin a new life? I don't know. Today everything fell apart, in total ruin, and I don't know what I'll do.

My love.

I'm leaving you today.

To walk away from a relationship

To walk away from a relationship. Pentti Saarikoski wrote in *Letters to My Wife*: 'I certainly liked the woman I lived with there. But even so, I couldn't live with her. She walked so slowly. I was always a couple of yards ahead of her in the street. And she never got angry with me.'

True, you were always angry, we always walked side by side, hand in hand, but even so we didn't manage to be together, or did we?

I walk out of the door, close it behind me, it's morning. Where should I go? Right or left? The simplest thing would be to make straight for the guest house, but I don't want the simplest thing, I want something else, something more difficult and new. But what do I want? I want to be alone. I want not to be alone. So run my thoughts as I walk, I turn to the right, not the left, not towards the city centre as usual, I walk in the direction that will take me out of the city. I've got money in my pocket. I'm a free man. I miss you already. I'm going in the wrong direction, out of the city, I could turn round at any time, go back, but I walk straight on. How many relationships have I walked out of? Break-up blue sky, thin clouds, like small type, like leave-taking letters, I write: walk. The day starts, the warmth comes, a gentle headwind and something within me turns. I could do with a beer. The guest house opens in an hour. It's a good place. I'm well-acquainted with my habits. I rarely surprise anybody. I walk out of the city and reach the cobblestones near Bergenhus Fortress, through the park. The sun is shining. The grass is newly mown, the lovely smell, a sudden pleasure. A gust of wind, the trees lining an avenue; they make sure that the park keeps its shape, that the world retains its meaning. The leaves on the trees are changing colour, moving towards autumn. I'm moving towards winter or spring. It's the summer, late summer, people are writing August. But I don't want to write a letter, I'll vanish in silence, without a word, no explanation; I haven't got one.

I love you.

And there are the stone steps leading to the fortress, the small wooden bridge outside the walls and the path down to the Nye Sandviksvei road. Two fighting dogs on the other side of a fence, I feel my instincts surfacing, the desire to hurl myself at one of these beasts of destruction and rip open its throat. I feel the fear. The instant hate; the animals' hate and my own, I hate that which hates. But once I've passed the dogs, my mood improves, I whistle. Twee-tee-tee. Twee-tee-too. I walk along the metalled road, here the road bends, sharply enough for me to see back, see the city I'm in the process of leaving.

A bend. That lovely arc between what has been and what's to come.

I love this bend.

I've rounded it many times. But today I'm here for the first time. That's how it feels. Perhaps because I'm not going back this way, perhaps because I'm alert; today I see the bend, I follow it carefully, every single yard of it, every single pace. It's my bend. A trampled leaf, pebbles, a desiccated snail, a flattened frog, small tracks; you're on the right road. You're on the road to something familiar and new. Like going through a door backwards, it's your house, your doubt, your way. You follow me like a shadow. We walk side by side, hand in hand, each on a different side of the city. I miss you. But now the bend is over and the road straightens out, it forks in two like an over-mighty river; something it just wants to do. I don't know what I want to do, but I follow the road up and not down, I go to the right and into Amalie Skrams vei. I spent a year with the philosopher here, he was the one who taught me to walk. He taught me to live in a house. I'd never been fond of houses, they were too large and unaccommodating. A house is demanding, difficult. One must learn to master a house. One must learn to dwell. I learnt, but didn't want it, I didn't want to live in a house. We argued about it, you liked living in large houses. I haven't got time to live in a house, I said, and besides they frighten me; all those doors, those excessive rooms, all that useless furniture, the unfriendly windows. I grew up in a small flat. My parents lived in a new modern flat because they spent their time working. When they weren't working, they had to rest. Central heating, lino, wainscotting and a caretaker, these are the conveniences that make it possible to rest. That make it possible to forget about dwelling. One dwells. One works. One rests. I was happy in that flat, I said. But you wanted to live in a house. And sure enough; I had to chop wood, feed the stove, knock down one wall, build another, plane the floor, repair a door, replace a window, I had to paint the house. I worked in the garden. I moved the furniture round, the house was big, we didn't know what to do with ourselves. I didn't write a single word during those years. What I need, I said, is a few hours of peace and quiet, a few days without plans or the need to do anything. What I need, I said, is a small room, even better a cubbyhole. A small, cool, untouched and undisturbed room where I can write. But there wasn't anything like that in the house. It was during this period, when I was living in a large house, that the philosopher offered me a room in his own house, he lived alone in a villa. Someone should have told me that I was on the wrong track, I might have ended up with a palace, a bit like Kafka's ill-fated surveyor, but the philosopher was mainly interested in putting me right about the good life. I discovered for myself that there is no correlation between the quality of ideas or writing and the size of the house you're living in. Rather the opposite. Maybe big houses produce big thoughts, but they aren't necessarily good ones. Certainly not. In my case big houses produce small thoughts. Where should the coffee table go? When is the right time to paint the outside of the house? Which paint should I choose? Who should pay the bill? Which books should I write to pay off the mortgage? A crime thriller? I had the plot within my grasp. I wanted to kill the woman I was with. It was during this period that I learnt to walk. In some senses walking is the opposite of living in a house. This certainly applies to wandering, which is an extended, voluntary or enforced walking experience, wandering is wished-for or unwished-for homelessness. Had I not, for a long time, wanted to set out on the road, without plans, just walking, in any direction away from that murderous house? Every day the philosopher walked to and from his office. He maintained that it stimulated his thoughts. Walking initiated the thought process, and the thoughts one thought while walking, were better than those one thought while sitting still, in an office, for example. He spent most of his time in an office. I sat behind his desk in the house where he lived. I wanted to walk. Not out and back, but right off and away, as far as I could go. And now here I am, after many small detours, walking past his house, straight on, up the hill past Sandviken Hospital and what was once called Dr Marten's Hospital, where my mother worked, as a medical secretary, for Dr Madland and Dr Lien, and occasionally for Dr Ose. From my mother I inherited a respect for doctors, particularly psychiatrists, and she taught me how to write. She gave me my first typewriter, it was a medical secretary's typewriter, I have no idea how many medical notes and reports it had written, but that machine possessed a madness all of its own. When my mother died I really did begin to lose my grip, I flew to London, took the train to Swansea and went on foot to Laugharne where I sat down on a bar stool in Brown's Hotel to drink myself into oblivion. It was a mystical journey. It was a desperate journey. I'd read Dylan Thomas' poem 'Do not go gentle into that good night' at my mother's funeral. A few days later I was on the plane; I didn't know how I was going to cope. In pure desperation I followed in the footsteps of a poet. From the hospital there's a path up to Skyttervei. Past the football stadium. Past the old Co-op. Low-rise blocks in two rows, a play area, childless. Parked cars, newly cut grass, asphalt, stairwells, silence, there's a special silence all about these blocks. A shadowlike figure with a stick, ascending the steps like a husband who has lost his wife, up the steps towards the high-rise block, it's the caretaker, Osberg, I recognize him. He lives on the fourth floor, we lived on the tenth, in the flat which now has 'The Larsen Family' written on the door. Joakim Larsen, father to Rune, who does the television programmes. I remember Rune Larsen as a tolerably good boxer, although his father was better, according to my own father, who was also a boxer, though no better than his son, and I've got testimonials to prove that. Beneath the high-rise block is an underpass to the backyard, where steps lead past the boiler room and the clotheslines up to the steep slope that divides at Jomfrudammen pond. The path descends again towards Lake Langevannet and follows the old post road to Åsane. The road is only busy in a couple of places with the stream of traffic shooting into the suburbs. A bridge is crossed. A farm is passed. Thoughts are no better when you're walking. You just think differently. What am I thinking about? I'm hungry and I need something to eat. At Åsane I stop at the shopping centre to buy some things. I buy a rucksack, good mountain boots, toiletries and a copy of *Julie, or the New Heloise*. I've made up my mind I'm going far.

A lonely wanderer's reveries

Well, why not begin with Rousseau, Jean-Jacques, who said in his *Confessions*: 'Never did I exist so completely, never live so thoroughly, never was so much myself, if I dare use the expression, as in those journeys made on foot. Walking animates and enlivens my spirits; I can hardly think when in a state of inactivity; my body must be exercised to make my judgment active. The view of a fine country, a succession of agreeable prospects, a free air, a good appetite, and the health I gained by walking; the freedom of inns, and the distance from everything that can make me recollect the dependence of my situation, conspire to free my soul, and give boldness to my thoughts . . .'

Rousseau wasn't the first to associate walking with ease of thought, but he was the first significant writer who reflects on what walking means; he imbues it with a romantic value: one gets closer to nature; to one's origins, and immediately one feels a well-being, a feeling of pure happiness, one is also free. The walker experiences freedom. He can choose his own road. And then it's good for the intellectual processes and the health to move about on foot. It's best to walk out of the city, out into the air, out into the countryside and out into nature: it liberates thought and brings good appetite. But what shall we eat? Jean-Jacques was nature's friend and advocate, but he was no vegetarian. We find an inn in the text, and imagine a fine meal with lots of good drink. So we aren't in the clutches of nature, we're a good distance away from the wilds: in other words we find ourselves somewhere in between. And this in between is the haunt of romanticism. We've enjoyed a good stroll out from the city but wild untamed nature is a fair distance ahead. We are somewhere in between the city and its opposite: wilderness. Here, in between, man is freed from the demands of knowledge and culture. We have deserted the theatres and museums and the art that adorn the ugliness of modern life. But we're not so far removed that we can't get back to the warmth of home and the evening's notes. We inhabit an idyll. A landscape where one pleasant view supplants the other. We can't see the city. We look out across a cultivated scene with farms and small country cottages. Here is an inn, a church with a steeple. 'Absolute silence,' Rousseau writes, 'engenders melancholy. It is an image of death.' But we can hear the birds and the stream which runs through the fields. Over there, a flock of sheep is grazing, and at just the right distance we can see horses and cows. But loveliest of all is the view of a small lake where the lonely wanderer has a boat waiting. He rows out alone with one oar and spends hours lying on his back in the bottom of the boat, until he exclaims in ecstasy: Oh Nature! Oh my love!

Jean-Jacques is fond of nature. It is, in a sense, his love. He loves nature like a woman. For Rousseau nature is first and foremost a concept. It is pure and unproblematic, devoid of conflict and impurity. For Rousseau nature is a notion of a better and more unsophisticated place for human beings. It seems that Rousseau sees nature as an absence of towns, of all he despises: vanity and debate, society and art. Gone are the streets and the noise, the bustle and all the insincerity; merchants and lawyers, journalists and artists. Gone are industry and technology. Here, without all that, man is in his natural state: 'he wanders about the forests, without industry, without speech, without a hearth, without war or ties. He has no need of others, neither has he any desire to harm them.'

The wanderer is, according to Rousseau, a plain, peaceful man. He is free. He has left the city, has left family and obligations. He has said farewell to work. Farewell to responsibility. Farewell to money. He has said goodbye to his friends and his love, to ambition and future. He is really a rebel, but now he has bidden farewell to rebellion as well. He wanders alone in the forest, a vagrant. He walks the roads, without too many belongings, he has taken possession of the world and its possibilities. He carries all that he needs in a sack on his back.

Jean-Jacques leaves the inn. The rebel and nature-lover, simply dressed in a long, light brown fustian coat above short breeches and long woollen hose. His shoes are thin but good. He leaves the inn. Now he must decide whether to turn and go home, or whether to go on a bit further. Jean-Jacques turns, he wants to get back to the house and his desk. No sooner is he back at home; he's borrowed a small palace from a rich lady friend, than he seats himself behind his desk by the window. Here, in *Meditations of a Solitary Walker*, he writes: 'When, therefore, I had sat down to describe my mental state in the most extraordinary situation a mortal man can find himself in, I found no simpler or surer way of achieving it than by making detailed notes about my lonely wanderings and the reveries that fill them when I allow my thoughts to run completely free and follow their natural course, unhindered and untrammelled. These hours of lonely meditation are the only ones in the course of the day in which I am entirely myself, and belong to me without constraint or diversion, and during which I can say that I am what nature has intended me to be.'

I should have had a trade

'Gradually as the reading of Rousseau's works proceeds,' wrote Voltaire, 'I am gripped by an ever more uncontrollable desire to crawl on all fours.'

Back to nature? The natural state, an animal, no, this isn't funny, no joke, it's serious: we want to go down. Down on all fours, go to the dogs. Forget the upright, everything we keep up, we want to go down and not up.

There is an eating place in Åsane, a small watering hole with simple meals and cheap drink, four tables on a worn parquet floor, lamps that obscure rather than illuminate; it's a difficult place to pass by.

I know the waiter, Christian, a Chilean, I taught him Norwegian many years ago, a dashingly handsome man, only interested in girls and quite useless at anything else, or so I thought then, but here he is, having found himself a trade. Some self-esteem. He puts the beer glass down on the table unnecessarily hard: 'And what's happened to you?' he asks.

Well, what has happened to me?

At regular and disconcerting intervals the thought occurs: I should have had a trade. I've chosen other things, rebelled, written and published books; I've travelled and done lots of mad things, but I've never had a trade. You don't know the secrets of a workaday life, I think. The conversations in the canteen. The office parties, the seminars, the colleagues! You've never—ever—enjoyed a national holiday either. No one has ever hired you or fired you, you've never been promoted or made redundant, you've never been sent up or down, in or out, pushed forward or held back, you have, quite simply, always been your own boss.

A trade. It really is about time. You're halfway through life, soon it'll be too late, if you don't grab the chance today or tomorrow, or at least before you change your mind, you'll have missed the boat, the work boat, or bus, and you'll be left standing there like some crank, some idiot; a man who can't get a job in any firm or undertaking.

But which trade? Journalist? Solicitor? Advertising agent or salesman? No, all these are just impossible, not to mention intolerable: too much money, too few scruples, suspect morals. There are too many immoral trades! But what about a postman, bus driver, teacher? No, you are forced to admit that these jobs don't appeal to you, in the same way that you've never had the least desire to become an actor, a politician or an editor. So we haven't got very far. The truth is that you want a trade, but there isn't any trade you want.

What to do about it? You consider. You begin again, from a different angle: you begin with desire. What would you like to do? What do you enjoy most of all? And is it possible to turn that into a trade? Yes, of course. Someone who enjoys thinking, does everything she can to become a philosopher. Someone who likes writing, does all she can to become an author. But you're already an author, and you have no philosophical ambitions. Your favourite thing, after writing and thinking, is walking. Surely you must be able to turn that into a trade: a vagabond. A vagrant. A drifter. A wayfarer. There have always been vagrants. But today it's a trade and a status that's in the process of dying out. At least in welfare Norway. And you think: someone ought to preserve this trade. Someone ought to shoulder this responsibility. Someone ought to save this freedom, this pride, re-establish this trade and its standing; yes, you will be a wayfarer.

Down the open road

What was it D. H. Lawrence wrote? 'The Open Road. The great home of the Soul is the open road. Not heaven, not paradise. Not "above". Not even "within". The soul is neither "above" nor "within". It is a wayfarer down the open road. Not by meditating. Not by fasting. Not by exploring heaven after heaven, inwardly, in the manner of the great mystics. Not by exaltation. Not by ecstasy. Not by any of these ways does the soul come into her own. Only by taking the open road. Not through charity. Not through sacrifice. Not even through love. Not through good works. Not through these does the soul accomplish herself. Only through the journey down the open road. The journey itself, down the open road. Exposed to full contact. On two slow feet. Meeting whatever comes down the open road. In company with those that drift in the same measure along the same way. Towards no goal. Always the open road.'

This high-spirited song of praise is corroborated by philosophy. Søren Kierkegaard wrote: 'Above all, do not lose the desire to walk. Each day I walk myself into a condition of well-being, and walk away from every kind of disease; I have walked to my finest thoughts, and I know no thoughts that are so heavy that one cannot walk away from them. If one sits still, the nearer one comes to a feeling of being unwell . . . Therefore, if one just contrives to keep walking, everything will turn out all right.' And Ludwig Wittgenstein in his little known diary: 'Christianity says: Here (in this world) you mustn't—as it were—sit, but walk. You must leave this place, and you won't suddenly be snatched away from here, but be dead when your body dies. The question is: how do you walk through this life? (Or rather: it's your question!) Because my work, for example, consists solely of sitting in the world. I must, however, walk, not simply sit.'

Even Aristotle subscribed to a Greek tradition that linked thinking with walking. Aristotle walked and taught between the pillars of the Lyceum, the pupils of his school became known as Peripatetics, from the Greek *peripatein*: to stroll. The Sophists walked from town to town and taught rhetoric. We know about Socrates' walks, within and without the city walls, he loved walking and talking, strolling and conversing, but when a thought really struck him, he would stop, and he might remain still for a long time, on one occasion he stood motionless for an entire night. The Stoics were named after the colonnades of Athens; the stoa, a path where they strolled and argued. So it was philosophy that established the connection between thinking and walking: Immanuel Kant took his daily after-dinner walk in Königsberg. There is a well-known circuit in

Heidelberg called Philosophenweg, after the route Hegel is supposed to have followed for his constitutional. We recall Nietzsche's comment about not trusting any of his own thoughts that had not been arrived at in the open air, whilst out walking. But writers, too, walked and wrote about walking. We know that Dante got lost, *The Divine Comedy* is a journey, a Christian continuation of Orpheus' descent into the underworld, a myth which in turn was echoed by the Troubadours. And poets are the ones who've done the wandering. It is sufficient to remember Hölderlin's rambles, Wordsworth and Coleridge's walks in the Lake District and in Europe, Rimbaud's frenetic jogging away from his native town, and Aasmund Vinje's many mountain hikes. Charles Baudelaire was a city perambulator, the king of all loungers (it is said that Baudelaire was often to be seen in the street around the block where he lived wearing his night clothes, he would stroll up and down in his pyjamas, and in that way the poet demonstrated that he had turned the outdoors into indoors; he must have liked the thought that the streets were his home. At the same time we hear that the poet's flat had the feeling of being outside, people came and went, the rooms were constantly populated by friends and strangers, women and men, at all times of the day and night, and Baudelaire must have liked the idea that he'd turned his flat into a street), and in our own time there aren't many authors who have travelled so much and so far as Bruce Chatwin. All through his writing life he dreamt of producing a book about the nomads, and in one of the notes for what was planned as a major work, Chatwin points out that the English word *travel*, has the same root as the French word *travail*: to work.

A trade. At last. With Bruce Chatwin walking becomes work, I think; it needs no application form, no qualifications, it's just a case of setting out, out of the door, at any time, straight ahead, in any direction whatever, down the open road, on two slow feet. It simply can't be that simple. No. Let me tell you about my first breakdown.

Wales. Swansea. The summer of '98. I'm planning to walk from Laugharne (where I visited Dylan Thomas' boathouse and garage study at the mouth of the Taf; ah, the herons, the cries, the pubs, the songs: 'Dark is a way and light is a place') in the south to Conwy in the north, the Cambrian Way in other words, reckoned by walking aficionados to be a hike of thirty days, and one of the world's most beautiful. Preparation: I've crossed Spain with a friend, slept under an open sky, in the forest, by the roadside and on the beach, I've trained myself to sleep in every kind of location. I've criss-crossed the mountains and fjords of western Norway, tramped on asphalt and gravel and grass along forest tracks and paths and post roads, climbed some of the peaks; toiled to the summit of Skålatårnet in a suit, scrambled up Galdhøpiggen in Doc Martens boots, crossed rivers and glaciers, walked through tunnels and towns. But all this was child's play. Now for the serious stuff. I'm alone, without any schedule, one month, two months, it'll take as long as it takes, to walk home, on through England, with or without money, perhaps I'll work on a farm, in a restaurant, who knows, I'm headed down the open road. It's raining. I set out from Laugharne in rain, dressed in the usual suit and Doc Martens boots, a black rucksack, insulating mat and sleeping bag and far too many books. I buy a waterproof, jettison some of the books and washing things; all unnecessary weight, on the Ousland principle, until I'm left with only the essentials and my pack hardly weighs anything at all. Everything's fine. But it rains. It rains for six days. Wales is wet and green, and I curse greenness and wetness. My suit is ruined, my boots are split, my legs ache and I curse this tough wandering life. I curse Bruce Chatwin, D. H. Lawrence, George Orwell, myself and all the others who have set me on this preposterous journey; isn't my place in front of a desk? Shouldn't I chain myself to my desk, as Kafka recommended, wasn't the idea that I should write books? Haven't I got a home and a kind of family? Didn't I long for a trade, something secure and normal, an income? The story of one of my insane ideas. I give up. Take the bus to Aberystwyth, check in at a hotel, find a waterproof pub, bereft of landscape and the colour green, and drink until I've forgotten that I'm a wayfarer. No. I haven't decided to give up. The more I drink, the more I decide to try again. But not in Wales. Not here where it's forever green and endlessly rainy, no, somewhere else. Let me describe my second attempt.

Staufen. Germany. Spring '99

Germany. Staufen. Spring '99. A friend and I are going to cross the Black Forest, from Staufen (where Faust made his compact with Mephistopheles) in the north, to Todnauberg in the south (where Heidegger had his famous cabin). I've bought a new old-fashioned suit, a Gypsy suit with a crease in the trousers, blue material with silvery-blue stripes, new Doc Martens, sunglasses, plus bandages and plasters; we're well equipped, well prepared; two bottles of dry German wine for the heat, a bottle of spirits as a sleeping draught, an assortment of pills for everything. Up and away! Up! Up from Staufen in thirty-three degrees of heat. Until the sweat seeps through the material and we can no longer tell clothing from skin, until our feet are one with our boots and the path: walking into the forest, becoming part of it, empty the bottles, fill the senses, listen to the birds, see the shadows, scent the trees, turn into nothing and walk yourself into the ground!

We eat. German sausage and coarse bread. Drink wine from bottles wrapped in wet newspaper. A good conversation. We discuss Heidegger. Heidegger and his cabin at Todnauberg where he was visited by Paul Celan and René

Char. Heidegger and Nazism. I say: Sartre took a wrong turn to the left. Heidegger went wrong to the right, that doesn't mean we should embrace the political middle-of-the-road, we should be extreme, radical, but we must avoid ideologies. Yes. But where are we going to sleep? We carry on up, find a hilltop; views in all directions, the dark forest, the lake, the paths, Deutschland, Oh Deutschland, we roll out our insulating mats, crawl into our sleeping bags, take a tot of the strong stuff, talk, and here in the heart of Europe, high up, we found the Slowness Party. We are against everything that moves too quickly. We're against aircraft, cars, fast thinking, express boats and intercity trains. We're for everything that moves slowly, and after a few pulls at the bottle we realize just how radical our party really is; we work out a manifesto, select the snail as our emblem. For slowness and laughter. Good night.

We're woken by the birds. The warmth from the rising sun. We eat a good breakfast, move on, down, then up again, towards Feldberg where the map shows an inn. We follow paths, cross meadows, the yellow expanses of grass, the clearings in the forest, and the sudden glimpse of hare and stag. We walk and talk, we walk in silence, we walk and think, over fences, through gates, along streams. A three days' march to Todnauberg. We reach the mountain village in the late afternoon, in a mist, give up the idea of finding the philosopher's cabin. Enquire of chance passers-by: Heidegger? I don't know him. Never heard of him.

They've never heard of possibly the most important philosopher in Germany since Kant and Nietzsche. They don't know who he was, here in the village where he stayed when he wasn't teaching at Freiburg. Martin Heidegger? We ask the hostess at the guest house where we've booked in to shower and rest our feet. Ah, that Martin, she says, he once gave my father a cigarette, my father was thirteen. Would you like to meet my father? Yes, we certainly would. Out with a bottle of wine. In to her father. The cabin is empty, he says, no one uses it. A television crew came from England some years back, but since then it's all gone quiet. No one asks about Martin Heidegger.

We find the cabin next morning. It's on a hilltop, hidden among trees and bushes, but we recognize it from photographs. To our great surprise we see that the shutters are open and so is the door. We retreat. No. We've walked for three days and now we're less than fifty yards from the famous cabin. We go on up, my head pounds like a heart: what if a lunatic lunges out and chases us away? And sure enough. As we approach the cabin, we spy a figure in the doorway. I shout that we're from Norway, that we've come on foot from Staufen, that I'm a writer and a wayfarer. The figure steps forward and out, proffers a hand and says: Heidegger.

It's his grandson. We introduce ourselves, are offered a cup of water from the famous stream, each find a boulder to sit on, talk about Norway and about walking; about his grandfather's walks and later about philosophy and particularly the art of poetry and literature. Yes, of course he knows Rüdiger Safranski's biography of Heidegger. He knows about the dressing down Thomas Bernhard gave Heidegger in *Old Masters*. We ought to take that scolding as a big compliment, he says bringing the conversation to an end. And where are you heading for now? he asks. We're moving on, I say.

On. We move on. As in a fairytale. But my legs hurt and sleeping out begins to take its toll. I propose that we put up at a hotel. I miss a bed and a television, the walls and the curtains; I miss the absence of birds and the outdoors. But the wayfarer ahead of me, my friend Narve, suggests instead that we cross the Italian border in the Dolomites. He wants to walk in the mountains, see the crazy rock formations, walk at altitude, sleep at altitude, start the real walking. We argue. I have to admit that I'm worn out, that I'm not a proper wayfarer yet, and that this is my second debacle. It finishes up with us taking the train across the border into Italy. But after two static days at a hotel, I feel the restlessness and the prickling; walking has got into my blood, I want to get out on the road again.

But now I've learnt that it takes more than a snap of the fingers to live like this, that it isn't easy to be a wayfarer. It takes adaptability and pluck, training and time.

We walk through the forests towards Asolo, towards the house where I stayed with my friend, Harold Costello, the author who never wrote. It was in that house that I wrote parts of my first novel, and I think to myself, as we walk past vines, olive trees, beehives and the hawthorn hedge: the circle is complete. The circle has just begun. This is the beginning. The beginning of the long road to becoming a wayfarer.

I leave the eating place, the watering hole at Åsane, walk out of the door, in new boots, made by Garmont, they're light green and go well with my suit, a navy blue suit with light stripes and flared trousers. A new white shirt and, most eye-catching of all, an orange sports pack that glows. I'm happy with this image of myself, walk purposefully towards Åsane church where I rejoin the post road. They say that Rousseau went on his jaunts dressed in a kind of Armenian costume; a leather cap and leather scarf, a home-spun jacket. There's a portrait of him in this garb, painted by Ramsay. The self-assured bearing, and the madness one glimpses about the eyes, rings true to the self-portrait he paints in his introduction to *Confessions*: 'I have entered on a performance which is without example, whose accomplishment will have no imitator. I mean to present my fellow-mortals with a man in all the integrity of nature; and this man shall be myself.'

But it's impossible to write the truth about yourself.

You write and hide. You cover yourself in language.

What Maurice Blanchot wrote about Kierkegaard applies equally to Rousseau: 'By constantly talking about himself to some extent and reflecting on the events of his life, Kierkegaard manages as a rule not to say anything essential about them and founds his greatness on withholding the secret. He reveals and conceals himself.'

The Armenian costume is a disguise, just as Rousseau's writing is a disguise. He doesn't seek solace in nature, he secretes himself in literature, behind a mountain of words. He invents himself and his surroundings, and that's the way it must be. Rousseau isn't different, he makes himself different, the author who makes us believe he's a child of nature, is the affected hero par excellence; an *agent provocateur*, an idler, a dyed-in-the-wool poseur: 'I know my heart, and have studied mankind; I am not made like anyone I have been acquainted with, perhaps like no one in existence; if not better, I at least claim originality, and whether Nature did wisely in breaking the mould with which she formed me, can only be determined after having read this Work.'

And when you've read Rousseau, you're full of admiration for Jean-Jacques the writer, the man seems even more inaccessible, almost detestable, but it's the reader's privilege that he never need greet his author: 'And so I am alone in the world, without a brother, without a neighbour, without a friend—and without other company than my own.'

Was it Rousseau who discovered loneliness?

It can seem that way. Like all great loners Rousseau dreams of companionship, and the more he thinks and writes about this companionship, the more lonely he becomes. It is writing that makes him enemies, writing that isolates him and makes him forlorn. But writing is also the Achilles' spear that cures the wound it has caused; writing enables Rousseau to populate his solitude with readers and idiots.

Rousseau treats his reader with the same hauteur and apathy as Montaigne in his *Essays*: 'Reader! This is a candid book. It tells you right from the start that my only object in writing it is personal . . . Therefore, reader, it is I, myself, who am the subject of my book. You have no cause to spend your time on such a trifling and meaningless subject. And so, Farewell!'

The origin of loneliness must be language, I ponder as I go through the farm gate where the post road rises towards Mellingen. It's a lovely road. It was once used to deliver post on foot. Isn't the letter the very symbol of loneliness? The writer. Alone at his writing desk. The farewell letter. The love letter. The yellow envelope one sticks down and entrusts to its fate. Letters aren't written to relieve loneliness, but to seal it.

These are the thoughts that turn in your mind as you walk alone along a post road. It makes me think of the letter Hölderlin wrote to the poet Casimir Ulrich Böhlendorff, just before he set out on foot to cross the Alps to Switzerland and later to France: 'And now: live well, my precious one! Until we meet again. I am full of leave-taking. It has been a long time since I cried. But it cost me bitter tears when I decided to leave my fatherland in such haste, perhaps forever.'

But Hölderlin wasn't away very long. The following year he was back at his mother's, 'as white as a ghost, emaciated, with deep-sunk, wild eyes, long hair and beard, dressed like a beggar'. All that walking hadn't done

Hölderlin any good, he was now edging towards the insanity that literary history describes as a long isolation: 'He shut himself away in what was called the Hölderlin Tower by the River Nechar at Tübingen. Here, the restless, mind-darkened poet spent the last thirty-five years of his life. Each morning at dawn he would go out and stroll around the garden for four or five hours. The rest of his day was spent pacing up and down his room, in eternal conversation with himself.'

Hölderlin admired Rousseau, and in 'Hymn to the Rhine' the philosopher appears as a diffident sage:

> But he whose soul
> like yours, Rousseau, is impregnable
> strong and patient
> calm of mind,
> and with that fine ability to listen.

Ah, well. Hölderlin didn't have the access to biographies that we have today. In addition, there were so many similarities between the two men that each saw himself in the other. What is notable about Hölderlin's walking, was that—in total contrast to Rousseau's remarks about the health-giving and thought-honing effects of foot travel—it broke Hölderlin physically and disturbed his mental health. This may be because Rousseau mainly went for short walks and confused the idea of travelling on foot with taking a stroll, whereas Hölderlin, who had travelled far, was scarred and exhausted by what he'd experienced in the course of his wanderings. We don't really know. What is certain is that walking for long periods is tiring. Anyone who has read about wayfarers and tramps, knows that vagrancy is tough. Anyone who has seen photographs and pictures of vagrants, can see that the life of a vagrant is hard. Anyone who has been on the road for several months, knows that roving is brutal and damaging.

You're homeless. You're sleeping out. You're a stranger and you arouse suspicion. You're dirty and hungry. You're alone, walking and walking, there's rain and wind, you sleep where you can, in barn or boarding house; what you own you carry on your back, your legs ache, shoulders ache, body aches, you long for a bed and a lover.

I pass a couple of farms, go through a gate, follow a stream and eventually get a view of the part of the city I've left behind. Åsane. Half the suburb is dominated by motorways and shopping centres, new buildings and estates; terraced houses and blocks and detached houses which look uninhabitable from this distance, thin and flat, like a stage set. And it's even worse when you open the front door of one of these houses and look into a home whose only distinguishing feature is that it resembles all the other homes; the living room with its television set and all its lamps, so much artificial light, the disagreeable warmth, all the superfluous rooms, the hostile furniture, this semi-temperate interior that speaks to us of our wasted work, our misused money, our dull lives.

The other part of Åsane stretches away to fields and wooded hillsides, old houses and farms, tractor roads and paths, trees and streams, flowers and grass; the long, sloping open land that glows in the sunlight. The old time and the new. The old time wasn't better than the new. The new time is no better than the old. One must choose, to the best of one's ability, how well one wants to live. But how can it be that all this money, all this prosperity, has led to an uglier landscape, a more impoverished architecture?

How can it be that we choose cheap solutions, quick solutions, that we think and build and create so badly with all this money? These are the kind of thoughts you have as you take the old post road at Åsane.

I want to write letters.

I am full of leave-taking.

I cross the hilltops and walk down towards the local prison at Breistein; those high walls; a tree, the shadow of the tree growing up the hard concrete wall. Two horses graze in front of the wall, as if all this freedom outside the walls, all this beauty outside, is speaking of how cruel it is to be locked up on the other side.

I walk past the prison and the Refugee Reception Centre, a play group, gardens and houses, a dog on a leash, a greenhouse; banks of flowers, a man in a garage, in his car, I see nothing but confinement here where I'm walking, past, quicker now, following the metalled road to the quay and the ferry that will take me across to Valestrand. On the quay I strip off and dive into the sea. Swim. I can see the ferry halfway across the fjord.

The perfect day

Lonevåg, a guest house, simple; small rooms, a bed, a table, a chair, it's as it should be, an abandoned room that will be abandoned. I put my pack on the floor, take out my notebook and write down the stretch I've done.

Outside the window I can hear noise and laughter, it's the sound of a party. A group of youngsters is sitting around a plastic table drinking beer. The end of the week. There is a special note in the waves of laughter, a sharp tone of impatience and anger; come on, boys, we're out of school, finished with the job, let's get drunk. I go downstairs, towards the terrace with its plastic tables and parasols. Sit down at one table. The other is occupied by the youngsters, boys and girls, in a circle around the table, they're drinking and smoking, sitting in a circle, fully self-absorbed. I don't envy them in the least. For an instant I feel an ache, a longing, I don't know what it is I'm yearning for. A circle, they're sitting around the table and I can't help examining each one of them, face, hair, hands, movements, the way they dress, just like other young people, and yet they don't look like anyone else. The sun goes down. The birds have found their tree. A car stops, some people come, one of the girls goes; the girl with the yellow sweater and the fair hair, a crucifix round her neck, leather ankle boots. She gets into the car. And suddenly, through the rear window, she looks back to where I'm sitting.

In the morning it's sunny, the light comes through the clouds, through the leaves and the tree on the other side of the window, in through the window, between the curtains and across the floor in a mote-shivered ray towards the bed and the pillow where it strikes my face. Through my eyelids initially. Stripes of light into the darkness of a dream and the images dissolve. The light turns to water, I dream of water and float up, break the surface, lift my head out; it's day. I wake up. Lie there in the bed floating on the remnants of my dream; it's the beginning of a good day.

Will today be the perfect day?

It's Saturday, I can do what I want.

I can stay in bed. I can walk back to the city. I can carry on down the open road. A blank day. A blank life, it lies there before me, I only have to go out of the door.

I go downstairs to breakfast; an egg, white bread, a bit of cheese, orange juice and coffee. I'm alone in the breakfast room. The place is staffed by no one, patronized by no one. I'm happy to be alone. These unpeopled rooms remind me of why I've chosen as I have; an empty house, an empty lounge, an empty room, they make me write.

For the first ten miles I follow the road northwards. Then I cross the rest of Osterøy island through a valley, a narrow path trodden between a low ridge and a forest of birch and aspen, a light, open forest. I'm using a map, I'll walk to Kallestad and cross Veafjord by bridge. According to the map book I've bought, I can get a bed at Stamnes. I follow the path, it's like walking in a different age; a pond with swans, a derelict country house. An abandoned farm and this path that weaves nimbly across field and fen. A day's walk through a deserted landscape, disturbed only by traces of what has been; a fence, an overgrown garden.

This landscape is reminiscent of the small places in Sunnfjord, the deserted crofts, returning to nature. An empty hay barn, a silent house, and yet it's as if something of life clings to these smallholdings, a sound? Didn't something move in the window? A face? The sound of feet? I remember a place in Lofoten, we'd gone there on foot and found it abandoned, seven or eight empty homes and an empty school; we broke open the door to find a place to sleep and discovered the classroom tidy and intact, as if the pupils had just that moment raced out of the door for their long anticipated holidays. A calendar on the wall told a different story. It was open at June 1977. Or that place at Sunnmøre, somewhere along the gravel road to Øye where water had flooded an entire settlement, and now the houses stood there, below the water, seemingly whole and undamaged, full of secret life.

I walk uneasily past the spot that is watched over by the past, and after the stiff climb I'm rewarded with the unexpected panorama of a landscape of farmhouses and animals. I feel a spurt of joy; life has only moved a couple of miles from the overgrown valley, across the high ground and out into the open country, to new and better houses, to roads and communications, to an easier life. I think of Hoffman's Baron von R., who went around collecting views. This view is neither spectacular nor unusual, it's such an everyday view, the sort you see so often, from any elevated spot in the country, that you cease to notice it. It's a view to my taste, I think to myself, it seems reassuring. I sit down on the grass, lean against my pack and light a cigarette. In one of his poems, Vinje extols his rucksack as his best friend, his stalwart companion, and it really is true, I've already become fond of my pack, and have even begun talking to the dwarf that clings to my back. I say: now we'll have a rest. Just at that moment I'm aware of a movement in the grass. Five or six yards from where I'm sitting, a body. I sense it more clearly than I see it, it must be a relatively large body, like a child's, something newly born. And sure enough, I get up and walk gingerly over, and there is a deer calf. It's lying with its eyes closed and its nose almost pushed into the earth. It's dying. Its head is covered with flies, a swarm of flies that have clamped themselves to its head. A nasty, dark cowl that's boring into the animal. But no wound, no obvious damage. The calf is breathing. What does it remind me of? I'm overwhelmed by an immense sorrow which is superseded by an equally great and unfounded rage; the flies must be got rid of. I shoo the flies away, am forced to wipe and pick them off. They're so engrossed in death that they won't let go, but I brush them off, every last one. And then I do something unexpected. I pick up the deer calf, place it over my shoulders and start to carry it down to the nearest farm. As I walk, I begin to wonder if I'm right to interfere, if I shouldn't have left the calf where it was, perhaps its mother was taking cover nearby, frightened away by me, I don't know, I start to feel uncertain, should I carry the calf down, or back to where I found it? It will die anyway, I think. It's almost lifeless, it's going to die, and you'll have to accept it, I say to myself. You must accept death, for various reasons it's important for you to accept death; there's nothing you can do about it, not this time either.

I carry the calf back to where I found it.

I give up the battle against death.

Take the burden from my shoulders and lay death from me.

My mother and Agnete, I lay them both from me with this deer calf.

I place the calf of its side in the grass and leave it. Set off down the slopes towards the farmhouses and decide to knock at the first door and ask for a glass of water.

I found a resting place

It's getting dark. I must find a place to sleep. I walk from Grøsvik and arrive at a strange place, a meeting of four fjords: Osterfjord, Romarheimsfjord, Eidsfjord and Veafjord. It feels like I'm entering a zone, an area with its own force where water is stronger than anything else; stronger than the mountains, more powerful than the forest, older than the grass, quieter than the road and the houses along the shore. The long thin fjord arms are stronger than the mainland, they carried all there was of freedom and dreams to the confined valley hamlets. There is a silence and a strength in this watery zone that makes me think how natural it is that fairy tales exist, that people really believe in Bible stories. Was it in such a place that Jacob wrestled with the angel? Was it in a place like this that Noah's ark came sailing in high among the mountains to find solid ground in a world that had become fluid? This area where the fjords meet radiates a power and a light; it's as if I might see something here that I've never seen before.

What could it be?

An angel? A unicorn? A sea serpent? The only thing I can see is a freighter gliding into the fjord. It follows me part of the way, floating at my side, quiet and disconcerting, as I walk along the fjord. Yes, here is my prehistoric monster, it glows in the dark, breathes in the water, pounds and hammers like a heart. The rain comes on. It hammers on the fjord's surface, on the tarmac, obliterating the thin demarcation between land and water. The sky is grey. The mountains are grey. Soon everything will be black. I follow the lights of the freighter, cross over the bridge to the mainland, and just as I get to Stamnes, I notice that the ship has docked at the quay. The little bed and breakfast is full, I have nowhere to sleep. I'm wet and cold. Hungry and thirsty. I go down to the quay, call up to the ship and the bridge, a woman and two men come out on deck. I ask if I can sleep somewhere aboard. Anywhere. No, that's not possible. The three are about to leave the ship. But they've got a car on the quayside, they're driving up Modal, they can give me a lift. I say yes to Modal; I'm heading that way, to the mountains.

And what happens in Modal is like something out of a fairy tale, just as I open the door and struggle out of the back seat, I see a mythical four-headed monster coming towards me. I recognize three of its faces, Tore and Hildegunn and Hildegunn's sister Elisabeth, plus someone who calls himself D. J. Modal. What a fluke; by coincidence, if coincidences exist, they're on their way to the wharf and the Sjøhuset to have a few beers. Do I want to come along? And what am I doing here? And do I need a place to sleep? Yes and yes again, and I'm on my way to Sunnfjord. On foot? Yes. It's snowing in the mountains, are you going in that suit? Yes. I see. Do you want a beer? I want two.

We sit in a corner by the window drinking beer. The rain strikes the pane; the long, narrow chink of a fjord is shut off by the darkness and disappears with the mountains. The darkness is thick and total, it's hard to imagine that it will ever be displaced, ever be carried away by the weak day, the cautious light. We sit in the light from the table lamps. Hildegunn Dale and her friends are back home in Modal for a seminar about the poet Olav Nygard. Asbjørn Aarnes is here. Eirik Vassenden is here. Yngve Pedersen. Øyvind Ådland. We talk about Olav Nygard and his poetry. And as we talk and drink, it's as if the little place we're sitting in loosens the thin invisible ties that have anchored it to rock and wharf, and we float imperceptibly out into the narrow fjord, towards a bigger place, a more important place. Now we're sitting at the centre of things, and if only Olav Nygard had written in English or German, he would, they say, have been an international celebrity, an important poet. Well, maybe. But isn't the great thing about Olav Nygard that he wrote so beautifully in his own little dialect? And so he's a small, insignificant poet with huge resonance for the few who can read him? The great thing about Olav Nygard is surely that he's a poet for the few, and the fact that almost nobody reads him endows his verse with a secretive power, as if it has gathered up within itself all the world's quietness and folly. It has become beautiful in the most difficult way, unseen and uncomprehended, yes, almost untouched, so that now, after all this time buried in silence, it has begun to resemble the landscape it comes from. The poems have been passed by, in the same way as we pass by a tree without really seeing it, without comprehending what it is we've left behind us. The tree and the poem have the same message: that we must learn to see. We must learn to read. And when we read Olav Nygard we'll realize that everything we're searching for, yearning for, is found here, right in front of our eyes, no matter where we are. It's hidden in the simple intimate things of our surroundings, in the everyday things we walk past.

We talk. We drink. We become high-flown, and the bigger the words, the smaller the place we're sitting in. It shrinks, reassumes its normal size and floats back to its usual place in the cramped valley. Our talk is so loud and florid that it's impossible not to notice we're shut up in Modal. But I have to admit I'm pleased to be right here. I can think of nothing better: sitting around a table with friends drinking beer.

Settling down. Resting.

Eyes closing, listening to the lulling buzz of voices. The sound of glasses. The smell of beer, the faint scent of tobacco, leaning your head carefully on your neighbour's shoulder; thinking that soon you'll be lying in a bed.

Breakfast with the Dales in Modal

Morning. Sun. The river's running straight through the house. I lay awake a long time listening to the river flowing in through the window and the door, in through the walls and down from the roof, it rose from the floor and filled my bedroom with water. I dreamt that I slept never to wake again, I became the sleeper, a body that couldn't shake off sleep, a face that was unable to open its eyes. In the morning I awoke soaked in sweat, as if I'd been fighting; I'd been fighting to raise myself out of the river, out of sleep.

Hildegunn Dale has written three anthologies of poems. The house she grew up in stands right on the river which once rushed fierce and strong down Modal, the river flowed freely out into the fjord, one arm of which stretches all the way to Bergen, but now the river has been tamed by dams and plants. It lights up houses in Modal and Bergen, cities in eastern Norway and Sweden. It's a beautiful thought, that this dark, closed-in community in the mountains of western Norway lights up houses and living rooms in other parts of the country. It's like poetry, as if Olav Nygard's visions have come true: the scenery of Modal shining and lighting up lives and dreams far into the neighbouring land.

The countryside has been disturbed. Large mountain tracts have been ruined by service roads and dams, by artificial lakes and pipes going in and out of rock and moss. Krossen, the farm where Olav Nygard lived, is quartered by power lines and pylons; singing threads of steel and light, sewing together a new landscape, a landscape that needs a new language.

Some of those who forge this new language are sitting around the Dales' breakfast table.

We're sitting round the table talking about writing. We talk about staying put. We talk about walking. Hildegunn is writing about women who have walked, Dorothy Wordsworth and Virginia Woolf. I ask her if Olav Nygard was a wanderer.

No, not really, he did walk in the mountains a bit, like everyone else, and he walked down from Krossen to here, which was the hub with a post office, store and boat connection. He walked here from Krossen and back again to the farm, that was a good distance, but he was no rover; when he wasn't working on the farm, he liked to sit still. A poet is someone who sits still. The motion in Nygard's poetry is almost always cosmic or spiritual, everything from small everyday observations to great, universal dramas. The poet observes the movements in nature, but the observer, the seer, is usually static, he's resting, sleeping or waking, he lies there stormbound under his own effect.

He wasn't like Hölderlin or Rimbaud?

He was and he wasn't, with Nygard it is the ideas and the yearnings that are on the move, he himself remains stationary, in the same place. Olav Nygard is the local poet, but just where that locality is I don't know.

A place with two suns.

With many suns. What was it Gunnar Ekelöf said to Olof Lagerkrantz: 'I live in another world, but you live there too.'

The poet isn't alone.

No, not quite, but almost, Hildegunn says and laughs.

And now you're writing a book about walking, Tore says to me. Tore with his sharp face, it reminds me of a bird, vigilant, calm, as if he's constantly on the brink of a sudden decision, but he keeps calm, waiting, for what I don't know.

Yes, I want to write a book about walking, I say.

That's a good idea, he says.

It is a good idea, I say, and that's why I'm stuck, I just can't write when I've got good ideas. Good ideas are about the worst things there are. They make me sick. Good ideas seldom turn into good books.

But does that mean bad ideas make good books? asks Elisabeth, Hildegunn's sister, who everyone says is like Hildegunn, although she hasn't got the same look, the look that's impossible to fathom even when she's looking at the same thing as us. The poet's look. Hildegunn's look. Elisabeth has eyes that resemble her sister's, a mouth that's similar, a face that's alike, but this similarity is nothing more than a big difference.

Good books have nothing to do with either good or bad ideas, says Hildegunn. Writing is opposing your own ideas; if I know what I want to write, and how to write it, I won't bother. The process of writing has to be open, and so it's important to uncover the structures of the book, get to the meaning of the poem, which often lies deeper than where you want to go with it.

Does that also apply to prose?

It should apply to all literature, says Hildegunn. There's a story about Tolstoy, who had an idea about writing a novel in which he would condemn an immoral woman. He wanted to show how terribly badly things could turn out for a woman and her family if she was unfaithful, but the novel he wrote was nothing like the one he'd conceived. The writing process led, against Tolstoy's will, to the lovely and tragic story of Anna Karenina. That's literature, writing our way to something we didn't intend, a beautiful monster, like Mary Shelley's Frankenstein, something we hadn't managed to think out beforehand.

To the mountains

Tore and Hildegunn want to drive me the first part of the way, up the steep service road. Large parts of mountain scenery above Modal have been destroyed by the hydro-electric plant, I sit in the back seat with my eyes half closed, I've seen it before, this new Norway, these small places with their industries and power-generation projects, they laid the foundations for our immense wealth, and my own free-dom. Tore is driving fast, in low gear, as if he wants to spare me the sight of a desecrated landscape, but it's nothing to me that the landscape is desecrated, I'm off, up into the mountains, and once I'm high enough, this area will be small, be smaller and smaller, until it's finally swallowed up in the endless mountain fastness I'll be walking in. We have enough mountain and wilderness. After little more than an hour's walk the mountains up here seem almost untouched, except for the summer farms and the way-marked path which will take me to Vardadalsbu, one of the Mountain Touring Association's self-service huts. When you've been in the mountains long enough, you're glad of these traces of human handiwork, a wooden bridge, a stone wall, a small farmyard; little crofts in the mountains which, despite being deserted, fill the walker's ears and eyes with sounds and pictures of people and animals, he feels almost like raising his cap and calling out a greeting. It's raining. I've draped a raincoat over my suit and rucksack, a brown cloth cap on my head, I like the image of myself walking alone in the mountains, past mountain farms and empty cabins. In *River Dreams* Hildegunn Dale writes:

> Only ruins remain:
> a couple of names, the eye's yearning for every-
> thing that stirs

Loneliness. A couple of names. When you've travelled long enough and far enough along your own path, you're left with one or two friends, a couple of names, and that's all. Anything more would be a sign that we'd lost our way, I think in the mountains. Thoughts change in the mountains. Thoughts gradually become fewer and more succinct as the mountains open up and get bigger. You think better when you're walking in the mountains. You make your mind up to be more difficult, less amenable, you think riskier thoughts here. More than two friends would be indecent, false, I think in the mountains. How many friends do I have? I had lots, but now I've got two. Two good friends. That's all. That's enough. Possibly I've only got one. Just one friend. That's the truth. I'm content. One good friend, like a lover almost. You think less cautiously in the mountains, mountain thoughts, I think and walk up into the snow, following the edge of a snow slope that descends steeply to a mountain tarn. If I should fall into one of these fissures, slip over the edge and into oblivion, it wouldn't matter to me. I walk through the snow, plod through the snow, cross a valley, and another river, a higher, swifter current, without bothering to look for a fording place, cross the river up to my waist in water, sensing the cold water and the powerful current as a possible ending. No anxiety, not yet. I follow the valley up to the right of the river, walking nonchalantly and thoughtfully, neglecting to follow the path, shouldn't I see the hut soon? It's marked on the map, a few miles up from the river, at the head of the valley, at the foot of the high mountains. A mist comes down. Everything turns milky and impenetrable, I walk straight ahead. Where am I going? Now the fear comes. It arrives like a cold paralysis, I stop, unable to move in all this whiteness. Mist and snow. Cold. As soon as I halt, I can feel the cold, my wet clothes. This idiotic suit. The weight of the rucksack, the dwarf on my back. We're stuck here, I say. The silence is complete. I am alone. Or am I, there's the feeling of some sort of presence, a bird, a hare, the dwarf on my back, something, someone, what? I look up, amazed that I can see clouds, a rift, strips of blue, a shaft of sunlight, it's clearing. The sun is breaking through. I stand there and wait. The mist lifts. Is snatched away. Driven away. Who's driving it away, a wind, a voice? I can't hear anything. Just as the mist thins I see the hut. Right in front of me, not ten yards off, the grey hut wall, like a flimsy stage flat, as if someone has turned a theatre set around to display a completely new scene. For a second or two it seems unreal, almost unnatural, but I feel how the fear is evaporating with the mist, how the sun strikes my face and suffuses my body like a wild, warm exultation. I take the rucksack off my back, embrace it, walk the final ten steps to the hut calmly, and clasp the dwarf tightly as if I never want to let him go.

Night in the mountains

How good it is to get inside: to go through the door, put your feet on a floor, stand by the living room door and look in at the stove and the table, the windows and doors, step through the living room, find the door to the bedroom; there is the bed, this is where I'll sleep.

Feeling the joy a house gives isn't the same as the satisfaction of owning one, the pleasure goes deeper, it comes from finding a place to rest, a place that's warm and bright, where you can cook and eat in peace and quiet, a place where you can sit down at the window and look out; you are inside. The joy of a house is the joy of being within. The joy of being outside comes after you've found a house, it needn't be your own.

I enter the living room, undress, hang the wet clothes over the stove; lay some wood, set fire to the good, dry birch sticks. The heat spreads like a blanket. I fetch dry clothes from my pack, the wine-box, a packet of cigarettes, notebooks. I sit at the window as usual. Eat, drink, smoke as usual. Make notes: I can write anywhere, all I need is a table and a chair. All I need is to be inside.

'Just make yourself at home.' I start, it must be the dwarf talking, he's imitating a familiar voice; my sister's, she is on her way out of the door, on her travels, she'll be away a few months, I'm borrowing her flat and immediately reorganize the furniture, dining table to the window, the best chair next to what has become a writing table. A workroom. Some years later, when that same flat had become mine, I never rediscovered, even for a day, the joy I'd felt during the two months I'd stayed there as a guest; the flat had become normal, taken for granted.

I'd furnished the flat with one sole aim: to write.

I wrote nothing in that flat. It was the best place I've ever lived in; a lovely, large, bright room full of books. There were books everywhere, on the floor, along the walls, in my bed, on my writing table, books in piles and rows; I wanted to read and write. I lived alone, it really was a lovely flat; a large writing table by the patio door, lamps, a good chair, sofa, cushions, wooden furniture; the room exuded a fine, solid stillness. Each day I sat at the writing table staring out into the room, rejoicing in the beauty I'd painstakingly built up; it was a perfect room. A perfect workroom. I wrote nothing in that room.

I've written all my books in flats and houses that belonged to other people, places that were lent or rented, usually for short periods, I haven't—for reasons I don't fully understand—ever lived in one place for very long. 'I cannot dwell,' wrote Rilke.

I've often wanted to dwell, but have never managed to. Whenever I've wanted to settle down, something has always happened to make me move. Just like Klaus Høeck, I dream of writing a book about all the addresses I've had; the streets, flats, towns, rooms, houses, all these impossible places we call home.

I sit by the window making notes. A clear darkness, translucent, illuminated by the moon. Snowdrifts, a stream, glittering. Cold. Starlit sky. The warmth inside, the light from the stove, restless shadows, moving about, as if the fire imparts life to everything that wants to stand still. Nothing stands still, stillness moves, sometimes inside, sometimes out, I sit here becoming uneasy about nothing. There's a radio in the hut, battery powered, after midnight there is classical music, Johann Sebastian Bach. *Ich habe genug*. Bach's music frequently makes me cry, always makes me give thanks, to whom I don't know. I'm at home in Bach's music, it's not a house, not an abode, and yet you feel secure inside this music, a space whose beginning and end we don't know, a little construct that must correspond to the eternity we carry within us. We own nothing. I have everything I need. I am content.

Ich habe genug.
Schlummert ein, ihr matten Augen.

But this music of Bach's, these Bach cantatas, leave me wakeful, I don't want to sleep. I like sitting up at night, and here in the mountains: a quite special way of being alone, so far from that loneliness we sometimes suffer in a city. When loneliness is sufficiently strong, we discover that we're never alone, there is always someone, in some place or other who is connected to us, we think of them, they think of us; where is he now, how is he faring while he's away? He was here yesterday, we didn't think about him, today he's away on his travels, and the further away he goes, the closer he seems, for a time at least, a week, a month; he travels, we keep him alive. But if he doesn't return, we'll gradually forget him. He'll disappear as far as we are concerned. Where did he go to? He went to Morocco to write, two months in Morocco, he'll be able to concentrate and work in peace. I miss him, he sent a letter: how wonderful it is to be missed. I'm coming back in February, it's hot and dry here, it hasn't rained since I arrived. We're observing Ramadan, eating before the sun rises, eating again when the sun has gone down, sitting on benches at the food tables in the market place and waiting, hungry, tired, irritable, the man next to me has his cigarette ready in his mouth, lights it the instant we hear the call from the minarets; the calls to prayer, they wash through me like a wave of happiness, there is a strictness and simplicity here that does me good. I feel at home. In Morocco? I don't understand him. He's been away for more than three months. He says he's living in the garret of a small guest house by the sea. An old Portuguese fortified town, he's not doing anything, doesn't write, doesn't read, walks about the town and is swallowed up in the throng of faces and voices. How good it is to be hungry, he writes. How good it is to eat, he writes. How good it is to sleep under an open sky, with no more possessions than can fit in his pack. He's happy. Is he alone? In the evenings he lies on a couch in a room dried by sunlight, swamped by the view over the sea, he smokes and has discussions with a Moroccan boy who speaks English. He writes that the boy is beautiful. The smell of burnt cedar from the fireplace, the earth floor, the rugs, cushions, peppermint tea; to rest, lie, dream, forget time, that jittery, miserable time we live in, he writes. He'll be back in April, in the spring, he writes. I'll be back in July, in the summer, he writes, but I'm no longer worried when he returns, I've found someone else.

It's night. Night in the mountains. It sometimes happens—when it's dark enough—that you suddenly catch sight of a face, it looms outside the window, apparently without body or feet, no hands, just a face, it lights up for an instant and is gone.

The stove goes out. Off with the lights, off with the radio, into the bedroom, up with the window, the sharp, cold air. Night air. Darkness. Silence. Alone. Down into the sleeping bag, holding the dwarf, a small, puckered body, almost like a child; it's sleeping. Close my eyes under the covering, no thoughts, no images, just sleep.

The sun's reveille

The sun's reveille, light is a trumpet poking through the window, someone blowing: get up! I stay in bed. Light a cigarette, get the Rousseau book out of my pack, read a few pages, pure pleasure: reading in bed in the morning. There's nothing pressing, I can stay in the hut, stay inside all day, read and make notes, move on in the morning. A nice cup of coffee, breakfast and back to bed. But the sun is shining. The sky is clear and blue, like a fanfare, sounding: go out and walk! On with my boots, my clothes are dry, make some sandwiches, pack on my back, out of the door, good-bye to the hut, and away. To three more days in the mountains, two nights in the Nordalshytten and Solrenningen huts. From Solrenningen there's a path to Ortnevik and Sognefjord. I cross bogs and grass, am pursued by flies and midges, watch birds fly up, the sound of grouse taking off, my heart beating, my legs walking; a walking rhythm, I've found it now. Walk, rest, eat, think, see. Drink water from the stream, ascend again to the snow and almost sail away across the plateau at an even tempo, as if my legs were working automatically. Effortlessly, easily, as if my legs were erasing the landscape and drawing a horizontal line onwards. It's like intoxication, perhaps it is an intoxication, an ecstasy of the body that eliminates climbing and effort, removes anxiety and pain, blisters that hurt, stiff muscles, the heavy pack, I notice nothing of all this, not until I stop, rest, briefly, I carry on walking. There is a point, a stage at which walking has broken through a definite barrier; you no longer have the desire to stop, you just want to go on walking, walking, walking, it doesn't matter where any more or why, in which direction, walking has got into your blood, an ecstasy, an ecstasy of freedom; you can go where you want, as far as you want, perhaps you'll walk so far that it will be hard to return to normal, to what was before, a job, a home? You're walking towards something new. When you've been walking long enough, you gradually feel that you've set out on a longer journey. Why cut it short, why not continue? To what? To where? To whom? You don't know. You walk.

I walk down towards Ortnevik. The little village way down below, and Sognefjord, an overwhelming sight, the tiny houses and the enormous fjord. The houses in a cluster around the jetty, a church, it reminds me of Ibsen's Brand, that insane priest, his landscape is here; the shadow of the mountains and the cold wind from the fjord, this is where he would live. It was here that he sacrificed his child on God's stone-hard altar; the old law: belief has its price, you must pay with suffering. Brand's God was also Abraham's God, Job's God, Moses' God, Jesus' God; he who sacrificed his son for something greater, it's hardly surprising he made the same demands of other fathers. The path descends steeply into Ortnevik. It's starting to get dark. Lights are coming on. Evening is approaching. I have heard and read about Anders Øvrebø, the mountain man, who lives at Ortnevik and whose house is open to other fell walkers. I hope he's still alive and that I can find him. I ask the first person I meet, a man with a dog, he points out the house, a small farm just behind the church. I ask what time it is, it's just after nine. Anders Øvrebø is alive, I find the house, knock at the door, it takes a while for him to answer. He's an old man with a young face, almost childlike, in whom the years, though they may have left his face unscathed, have set their mark on his body instead; he walks slowly, and with a limp. I turn in every night at ten, every night at ten, it was a good thing you came before ten, he says. He shows me into the house, we go into the kitchen, a blue room, the radio is on, he gets a key out of a cup, looks at me as if only now noticing that not everything is as it should be: have you crossed the mountains in those clothes? he asks. Is he suspicious, wary? No, he gives me the key, accompanies me across the farmyard; ah, you look like we used to fifty or sixty years ago, cap and suit, it reminds me of the old days. We enter the farm cottage, in the living room there's a wood stove, three bunk beds with woollen blankets and pillows, a small table by the window. I go to bed at ten, he says, but I'll talk to you early tomorrow morning, eight o'clock. Then he leaves the room; his steps and movements bear witness to the fact most of his time is spent alone; I'm just a small body in all this loneliness, a small guest, an almost imperceptible visit. In the adjoining room there is a single bed, a smaller stove, I light it. Undress, get into bed, pull the Rousseau book out of my pack, read a few pages, there's nothing like reading in bed at night, before going to sleep.

With Anders Øvrebø at Ortnevik

At seven-thirty there's a knock at the door, breakfast in the
kitchen at eight. Anders Øvrebø sits at the breakfast table
with the radio on, as if he's on the lookout for something
new and that this novelty might pop out of the radio at any
moment. He asks me what things were like in the mountains, is keen to know small details, the amount of snow, if
I saw many birds up there, did I meet any other walkers?
No. None. Walking alone in the mountains is best, he says.
How far have I come? From the centre of Bergen, I reply.
And how far am I going? I don't know for certain, I'll cross
the fjord for a start and visit Ivar Orvedal at Måren. The
poet? Yes. Are you a poet, too? No. I'm an author. And have
you written many books? I've written eight books, I say and
try to move the conversation on to something else; is it a
long time since you've been in the mountains? I ask. He
shrugs his shoulders; I can't really remember, he says. I sit
there wondering if this is vanity, he seems vain, and
reminds me in a way of Sviatoslav Richter, the large head
and the feminine face, the coarse neck, wide throat, and
yet long arms and beautiful hands which he holds in the
strangest poses in front of his nose and mouth. I've seen a
film of Richter going round Odessa, the way he walked

fascinated me, I don't think I've ever seen anyone walk so beautifully. Anders Øvrebø is seated, but his arms and feet are moving, it's as if he's walking away as he speaks, in short spurts, he doesn't say a lot. He talks and moves away, becomes more distant and finally vanishes behind a ridge. A few minutes later he re-emerges by the kitchen table: what were we talking about? he asks. About the mountains, I reply. Yes, I've got great respect for poets, he says and in that instant I realize that we're alike, he and I, in the sense that neither of us wants to talk about what we know best. We sit studying each other, he looks at my footwear, studies my trousers and the cloth of my jacket, as if searching for himself, it may be that he's thinking: this is how I would have dressed and behaved sixty years ago. Well, it's time you were off, he says, as if it's a decision about his own movements. He gets nowhere but is always on the move; there's a boat at ten, he says.

I walk down to the quay and find a shop, I buy some beer for Ivar and me, some cigarettes, a newspaper, that's not for me. The boat, a small ferry, arrives, it carries no passengers or cars. I'm the only passenger, I go aboard, buy a ticket to Måren. It's three years since I was there last, three years since I did a reading at the Måren Festival. Ivar doesn't know I'm coming, he may not be at home, in which case I'll have to cross the mountains to Vadheim. From Vadheim I'll follow the old post route to Sande, from where I can take the road to the family cabin at Sygna, two or three miles from the farm of Osen at Bygstad. I board the ferry, stand on deck thinking of Richter playing Bach: *Das Wohltemperierte Klavier*, preludes and fugues; Richter's hands singing and walking, they walk down a road I don't yet know.

Boots and the Man, I sing!

'Boots and the Man, I sing! For you cannot tramp without boots. The commonest distress of hoboes is thinness of sole . . . Two friends set out last Spring to tramp from Bavaria to Venice, luggage in advance, knapsack on shoulder. But they had not the right sort of boots, and they lingered in the mountain inns quaffing steins of brown beer to take their thoughts away from their toes. They are in those mountains yet.'

So wrote Stephen Graham in *The Gentle Art of Tramping*. He rounded off this sally with an exclamation: 'You should have leather-lined boots with most substantial soles.' I'm walking on a road, on tarmac, my feet hurt and I curse the tarmac, it saps the strength. Tarmac is the worst of all surfaces to walk on, worse than rock, worse than mountain, tarmac is hard and dead, I feel the concrete-like tarmac punishing my back, all the way up to my shoulders and neck, it goes to my head, fills my thoughts with black tar, and after five hours on a metalled road it's impossible to think of anything but tarmac and how to avoid it. I walk on the verge. Bjørvik, Sagevik, Halsnes, Holmelid, Strandenes, the further out along Dalsfjord, the saltier the water, I see the kelp at the water's edge and get the urge to bathe. Throw myself into the water. Swim in the reflection of clouds, of mountains like Laukelandshesten and Fløyen. When I see the waterfall of Laukelandsfoss, I long for a lover. But I have a lover and I've just left her. I've been on the road for nearly two weeks. Walked all the way from Bergen to Ivar at Måren, three nights at his house, two nights in the cabin at Sygna, today I got up early and set out for Bygstad. I did some shopping at Bygstad, three new pairs of socks, plaster for blisters, some cans of beer and cigarettes. Substantial soles don't help on tarmac. My feet ache and sting, I kick off my boots, and my clothes, dive into the fjord and swim. I recognize the taste of meltwater and salt, that taste of the western fjords caused by the meeting of rivers, streams and waterfalls with the sea. A portent of ocean. I'm on my way to the ocean. I rest and dry myself in the sun, lie in the grass and fall asleep. When I wake up it must be afternoon, I eat a bit of bread and sausage, drink some beer, a simple meal, I'm content. Move on towards Dale and yearn for a forest floor and grass, bog and earth under my feet. I walk through four tunnels, pressing myself against the wet cold rock wall each time a car whizzes past. I miss mountain and forest, and yet there is a particular joy about heading towards a built-up area, past the service station, the first terraced houses and gardens, past the shops and windows, the knowledge that here I can eat and sleep.

I find the old sexton's house, behind the church, where Jakob Sande grew up, now they let rooms named after his poems; I'm given the room called 'Sleeping Woman'. A room with two beds, a bedside table, reading lamp, crocheted curtains in windows with a view over a large flat field. A good room. I wash and shave, a clean, new, white shirt, dress and walk to the inn, an old two-storey timber house, which is by the quay. A table by the window. I order a bottle of wine. A good meal with potatoes. A cup of coffee, cigarettes. In a half circle around my table: a group of women. They're going to the Mediterranean, they talk about the Mediterranean, Mediterranean beaches, the sun, the heat, they're in the Mediterranean already, running about half-naked on the beach. And in the innermost corner, in the half-darkness, three men. Three musicians, it turns out, from Voss, but originally from Sunnfjord, it turns out, on their way to Haugland, it turns out, a gig at Haugland. I introduce myself. Yes, we drove past you walking along the road, says Per Indrehus, it reminded me of something, something from the past, nobody walks the roads any more, he says. No tramps, no Gypsies, no wayfarers, they've all gone, whatever happened to them? The hay has gone from the barns, the refuge for the homeless have shut, just like the brickworks. The roads are tarmacked and the car has destroyed the slow life, the entire modernization process in Norway must have got rid of the itinerants, says Indrehus. I can remember Rottenikken, Indrehus says. And Henrik Larsen. Musicians walked the roads, and then there was the author Hans Aleksander

Hansen, a friend of Prøysen's, he was a hobo and a bum. The young Jakob Sande was a tramp and a seaman, but he ran aground in Oslo, says Indrehus, he got wrecked in the capital, in the fashionable West End, as a teacher, among strangers, he went under and drowned. In the summer he'd come ashore at Kobbeskjeret, but there he drowned himself in alcohol, he sank and drowned, singing, right outside his cabin door, says Indrehus; he bawled and sang so loudly they could hear him all the way to Lending. They could hear him all the way to Espedal, I say. The lights flash on and off. Are they flashing the lights? asks the singer; I don't believe it, is it closing time? It's bedtime, says Indrehus. But we sit out in the yard in front of the sexton's house, with cans of beer. And then there was Aasmund Olavsson Vinje, says Indrehus, he was a wanderer and a poet, he dreamt of leaving the capital too, for the thought really is father to the man.

> And so to the hills
> like a bumpkin I'll take,
> to find those I know
> and myself quite forsake.

Yes, *Remembrance of a Voyage*, says the singer, that's the soberest book in our literary history, it's got such a dry and unsatisfying ending. Vinje wrote:

' "Ah, this land, these mountain valleys," a man said to me, "Ah, this land! A land fit for angels."

'"If so," I retorted, "the angels definitely don't eat enough."

'"Hmm!" he replied " . . . well, we certainly haven't got as much corn as Denmark has, but . . ."

'"But," I put in quickly, "we have men who can eat corn." '

You see! says the singer raising his beer can, Vinje should really have written:

'But we have men who can drink corn.'

At the hairdresser's

To wake up alone beneath a thick white duvet, on a perfect pillow, to wake early, lie there waiting for the right moment to get up; perhaps when the sun strikes the foot of the bed, or later, when the sun has found my face and left it. Postponement. Until I suddenly get up and am hit by the hangover, it settles in my neck, tugs at my hair and beats at my temples. I put up no resistance, go into the shower, what I need is a good breakfast and a cup of coffee, what I need is to get out on the road again, walk off the remnants of the night and the alcohol. There's a bakery cafe in the centre of Dale, homemade bread, freshly filtered coffee, newspapers, a table by the window. From the window I can see the bus station and the bank, the people who walk past, a face, hands, the way she walks and how her hair flies in front of her, towards the churchyard and the white church; it throws a pointed shadow at a square of light where two girls are playing with a ball, the sun and the ball, I am gripped by an old, inexplicable fear, the sun and the ball, the unquiet shadows, I get up quickly and go out.

There's a hair salon in the shopping centre, the usual interior; a row of mirrors and chairs, basins and shelves with scissors and combs, the pleasant lighting, the nice, clean smell, the sound of clippers. The soothing conversations, the buzz of voices, I sit down to wait, leaf through a newspaper. There are three girls at work, I sit and wait for one of them, the prettiest, that's the way I am.

Having your hair cut. Shutting your eyes. When you open them again, you are altered. The feeling of being keener, cleaner and older.

The feeling of being new. You're the same person in a new way. It's evident that you're older. The short hair makes your features more pronounced; that large nose is growing. The haircut has emphasized your eyes, they grow out of your face like two light-sensitive flowers; blue iris and lilies: the soft, leaf-shaped mouth with scars from fights and injuries, your past, how it is slowly evoked in the mirror. When I was young I had an ordinary face, it could be used for anything, so it seemed. It could be whatever it wanted, it was an insignificant face. Only when it began to be injured, after all the fighting and boxing, did my face assume an air of being limited; it tapered, became harder, resolute. I determined to destroy the potential of my face, I wanted it to be an unsophisticated face. A face like that changes all the time, it doesn't set, it doesn't fall asleep, sometimes people don't recognize it.

I've never enjoyed having my hair cut, but even so I get it cut so often that it's almost an obsession: off with that hair. Like when you try to get rid of a person who's followed you all your life. But the more often it's cut, the more often you look like yourself. Therefore you let your hair grow, beard grow, I try a pair of glasses. New clothes, a jacket that's a bit too large and trousers with a crease, you put on a few pounds, fill out and change your walk, you move more slowly and ponderously. You don't swing your arms. One day you buy a hat, you never take it off. The hat becomes part of your head, it sticks to your hair. Now it's time for a haircut. You go to the barber. It's in Istanbul, in one of the side streets, a mean, dirty little shop, where people come who have nothing to hide. A naked face. A naked head, you shave your hair off.

If you're going to walk to Haugland, she says, do make sure to take the forest road. Follow Dalsfjord out to the last farm, go through the farmyard and follow the old access road until it meets the forest path, it's signposted and marked, you go up through the forest and out along the ridge until you see the centre of Haugland and the water. It's a nice place.

A nice place. What does she mean by that?

I walk along the edge of the fjord again, newly shorn and in good spirits, a sandwich and a bottle of water in my pack. She was gorgeous, I say, confiding in the dwarf. I've got her card and name here, she gave them to me, opening times and telephone number, why did she do that? I'll never get my hair cut there again.

Silence. The sound of footsteps, they're my own. I've been alone too long.

I'll phone her tomorrow, it's Saturday, well, why not? I've got nothing to lose, she can only say no, it makes no difference to me. It would be best if she said no. Most likely she'll say no, I say, of course she'll say no, give me the bottle of water. I walk past the last of the farms, past the garden and the fruit trees, through the gate and across the meadow, another gate and up through aspen and birch, the pleasant shade on the steep bits, a good, soft carpet; I walk beneath a spreading roof of leaves.

It's a relatively short walk. I eat at the top, rest my back against a rock, it's warming, an embrace, I press my neck into the cleft, rest my hand against the damp moss, poke my middle finger in and close my eyes: you've been alone too long, I think.

Faun's evening

It's Saturday and I ring the hair salon. Ask for Janne.

You cut my hair, you cut it yesterday, I've walked your route to Haugland, I say.

The words flood out of me, a great gush of words, as if I'm trying to drown her. I can hear her doubt, that little uncertainty that turns into resolution; she says no. We could swim, I say. We could swim and eat and go for a walk. We could talk. Don't say no. Say yes, I say. After a long pause Janne says she'll have to think it over. Ring back in half an hour. I ring back after twenty minutes. What do you say? I ask. She says something or other, I can't hear what. She hesitates, she makes conditions, she says . . .

Of course, I promise, I say and make her a promise I can't keep.

Janne. She arrives by car, a silver-grey Toyota Corolla, dressed in denim jeans and a white blouse, brown boots. She's hiding behind a pair of sunglasses, her denim jacket is too small.

I follow her up towards the cabin watching the long legs and the slim back which is carrying a small pack, take off your pack, I say. She places it on the floor and I show her the cabin; the little living room with a wooden sideboard that functions as a kitchen, a small bedroom, bathroom and terrace, that's all.

We sit on the terrace, talking, she speaks and interrupts herself with questions, she says: I'm twenty-six. How old are you? She says: I'm studying in the evenings. What work do you do?

I shouldn't have come, it's a weakness I have, I just can't say no. I should have said no, shouldn't I? I liked your face, and your hair, sometimes I stand there snipping, and suddenly I think that I'm the one creating the face, it's my face, I could have ruined it, I could have been wicked and cut those looks to pieces, but I don't do it, and when I succeed, when the cut goes well, I think how it's down to me that she looks better than she deserves.

What do you think of hairdressers?

That they're superficial? That they throw away their lives on something idiotic? We snip and snip but after only a few weeks the hair has grown out again, and after just a month the hairstyle is ruined. It's like a garden, it has to be maintained. I think I'm a kind of gardener: off with whorls and stray hairs, off with knots and unsightly growth. But hair grows. That impossible battle with hair. The everlasting battle with hair. Mine's the oldest profession in the world, she laughs.

I'm a Christian and I had a Christian upbringing. A good, strict upbringing, but that doesn't help, I've got a weakness, almost a defect, a catastrophic defect it's almost a disease: I can't say no.

Janne. She talks. The shadows on the terrace lengthen. She wants something to drink. That wide mouth, those blue shadowed eyes. She drinks. We don't walk. We don't swim. We forget to eat. I sit with Janne and listen. At first with my ears, then with my eyes and soon with my whole being. I listen with my hands. I listen with my brow and mouth, with my tongue and fingers.

I hear how she moans and cries.

I hear how she breathes and how she holds her breath.

Breathless. Silent. Almost dead.

And then she comes.

Janne.

She shouts my name.

I don't know her.

She falls asleep with her clothes on. Her boots stick out from under the blanket she's pulled over her. It's morning. The sun is coming in through the window, lighting up the curtains and the lamp by the living room table. I have been down for a swim. Make breakfast, filter coffee and toast bread on the cooker ring. She wakes, begins to cry straight away, she says: you promised me. You promised not to touch me. You promised to be careful, we were going to eat and talk and go for a walk together. I've got a boyfriend. And I've got a huge weakness, a terrible defect. If anyone feels me or touches me, in the wrong way, I simply surrender. It could be almost anyone, I must be ill. Janne says: I've got to get back. I'll drive back and you'll have to disappear. As if this never happened. It hasn't happened. We must cut the whole thing, forget it.

To go alone or with a companion

I wake up by my rock, half lying, half sitting, how long have I been asleep, the sun is going down; it's early evening. I've done a round trip and am heading back towards Dale, I want to take the ferry across the fjord, from Dale to Eikenes, I want to carry on down the road to Askvoll, towards the sea.

Part of the old post road between Bergen and Trondheim, restored and waymarked, passes Flekke and Dale, walking it gives me no pleasure, I can't even remember the route, nor the landscape, nor the farms and vegetation, I remember neither trees nor mountains, pay no heed to my surroundings, I just think about Janne.

Back in Dale I phone a friend. He lives at Førde. He's got access to a cabin at Fure where we often go to rest and read. He'll meet me at Askvoll, in the evening at the pub in Askvoll. I take the ferry from Dale to Eikenes. Get a lift from a fellow passenger as far as Holmedal, he advises me to take the old road from there, along the fjord past Vik and Vårdal; it's a lovely walk, he says, revving up and driving away. It is a lovely walk. But the tarmac is beginning to cause my feet serious problems; they have become two large blisters, each step is painful, burning as I walk. It's so good to sit down, lie down in the grass and rest. Raise my feet: they're pounding like a heart, walking in the air, they don't want to stop, a walking machine, they're walking and pulsating. I lie for a good while in the shade. Change plasters and socks and carry on along the road. My feet are bleeding. After a few hours pain is the norm. I walk like an injured animal, hobbling and hopping, limping and stopping, but in one way the pain is good, it reminds me that I'm moving under my own steam and that walking has its price: I pay with my feet. I walk towards the centre of Askvoll, I'm grateful for every yard of sand and grass, I walk along the beach, rinse my face in salt water and sense the great joy of arrival: I've got here.

The guest house is by the jetty. There is a pub on the ground floor. A long wooden bar, two beer taps, shining, the light from the sun and the lamps. It will get dark. It's just a case of ordering something to drink, taking a seat by the window, watching the people go in and out, women and men, old and young. There's a billiard-room in the innermost recesses. Music from the speakers, just get out the notebooks, write and drink and wait.

In his essay 'On Going a Journey', William Hazlitt discusses to what extent it's best to go alone or with a companion. He decides it's best to go alone: 'I cannot see the wit of walking and talking at the same time.' Hazlitt extols being alone, freedom, being able to go where you want, at your own pace, merge undisturbed into your surroundings, think your thoughts deeply and without interruption: 'No one likes puns, alliterations, antitheses, argument, and analysis better than I do; but I sometimes had rather be without them.' For Hazlitt the walking trip is a quest for tranquillity and pure sensation, he wants to feel, think and become himself again. Walking is a kind of purification, you get rid of the dross and disturbance which others have deposited on you. He who walks is in the very best of company, he's alone with himself. 'One of the pleasantest things in the world is going a journey; but I like to go by myself. I can enjoy society in a room; but out of doors, Nature is company enough for me. I am then never less alone than when alone.'

However, anyone who has walked long and far knows just how necessary it is to walk with someone else at times. Some of the most demanding trips I've been on would never have been completed without a travelling companion. You don't cross Turkey alone. And if you do, you feel exposed, always insecure, often losing the feeling of freedom if you walk alone. Much time and energy is spent searching for safe places, places where you can relax and rest. A secure place to sleep. You become cautious, wary, always on the lookout. You avoid certain places and houses, you don't do the leg you want to do, curbed by fear you take precautions. When there are two of you, it's easier to sleep outside, under an open sky, during the day you walk apart, alone, but together; you encounter stray dogs, strangers with an assurance you never feel when you walk alone. William Hazlitt was a romantic, he took his walks in safe surroundings, most frequently in the Lake District, often in the company of Wordsworth and Coleridge, preferably alone. But anyone who crosses frontiers and wants to walk far will set great store by going with someone else, particularly if, like me, he has found the perfect partner.

Narve Skaar and I have walked in Turkey. We've walked in Greece and Romania, Italy and Germany. We've travelled together in Hungary and Bulgaria. We've walked through mountains and cities, crossed borders and countries. We've done short walks and long walks. We've sat in pubs and bars and studied innumerable maps in order to plan all the walks we want to do: the Cambrian Way through Wales, in St Paul's footsteps from Ephesus to Damascus, across the Turkish mountains to Armenia and Iran, the Atlas Mountains in Morocco, the Pyrenees, the Dolomites, the Andes and the Rocky Mountains. For Narve Skaar is a mountain man above all else; he prefers going up rather than down. He prefers walking at altitude rather than at low level. Only when the going starts to become testing, when it starts to get tough, does he find his natural rhythm and his best spirits. He has turned carrying the least amount possible into an art form; a couple of books, a spare white shirt, underwear and washing kit, a torch and a knife, that's all he carries. He owns practically nothing. His house is almost bare, apart from a stereo system, two lamps and a bed. The bed is situated under some stairs, which gives the sleeper a feeling of security.

William Hazlitt wrote his essay on walking in 1821. As a seventeen year old, during the winter of 1789, he'd walked the ten miles from Wem to Shrewsbury to hear Samuel Taylor Coleridge preach to his new congregation. The meeting with Coleridge made an indelible impression on the young Hazlitt but, after many years' friendship, his youthful admiration had turned to an acute, if amicable, repugnance; each time Hazlitt described his friend he would employ sarcasm: 'His mouth was gross, voluptuous, open eloquent; his chin good-humoured and round; but his nose, the rudder of the face, the index of the will, was small, feeble, nothing—like what he has done.'

Hazlitt couldn't help remarking on Coleridge's gait; it was a manifestation of the poet's fickle political affinities and his quixotic character. Hazlitt remained a radical and a revolutionary all his days, Coleridge became wedded to a conservative and reactionary view of life, accompanied by vacillation and resignation: 'I observed that he continually crossed me on the way by shifting from one side of the foot-path to the other. This struck me as an odd movement; but I did not at that time connect it with an instability of purpose or involuntary change of principle, as I have done since. He seemed unable to keep on in a straight line.'

Despite his way of walking and their political disagreements, Hazlitt and Coleridge remained friends. In his essay 'My First Acquaintance with Poets', which he wrote twenty-five years after his initial meeting with Wordsworth and Coleridge, Hazlitt tells how the poets taught him to think and see, write and walk: "Coleridge has told me that he himself liked to compose in walking over uneven ground, or breaking through the straggling branches of a copse-wood, whereas Wordsworth always wrote (if he could) walking up and down a straight gravel-walk, or in some spot where the continuity of his verse met with no collateral interruptions.'

The poets wrote as they trudged along, over rough or flat ground. William Hazlitt did his walks with Rousseau's books in his pack, he made his notes, wrote his essays, and these sallies laid the foundations for a genre of his own: wayfaring books. In the years that followed Robert Louis Stevenson wrote his *Walking Tours*. Leslie Stephen wrote *In Praise of Walking*. John Burroughs *The Exhilaration of the Road*. Stephen Graham *The Gentle Art of Tramping*. Over in America, Henry David Thoreau wrote the essay 'Walking': 'If you are ready to leave father and mother, and brother and sister, and wife and child and friends, and never see them again—if you have paid your debts, and made your will, and settled all your affairs, and are a free man, then you are ready for a walk.'

In the autumn of 1855, Walt Whitman gave his own book *Leaves of Grass* good reviews in three separate publications. Whitman wrote of Whitman that *Leaves of Grass* was a shameless child of the people. No imitation, but a product and an idiom of America.

A few months later Whitman received a visit from Henry David Thoreau who had travelled from Boston to Brooklyn to see this 'wild man'. Thoreau was surprised to be received by a polite individual, clerkish and well-dressed. Thoreau found that once he'd met him he was no longer disturbed by any of the bragging or egotism in his book.

Whitman was dabbling in the building industry at the time. He allowed himself to be portrayed for the anthology dressed in workman's clothes, his shirt open at the collar, wearing his hat at an angle and looking the very picture of a tramp and wayfarer. The longest journey he would ever undertake was from Brooklyn to New Orleans. His friends described him as a man of habit, fond of home, someone who would be loath to leave his usual circle and daily round. Nevertheless, it is the fictional character, the man in the photograph; the vagrant and vagabond who I imagine writing the lustiest and most invigorating of all travel poems, 'Song of the Open Road':

> Afoot and light hearted I take to the open road,
> Healthy, free, the world before me,
> The long brown path before me leading wherever
> I choose.

Henceforth, I ask not good fortune, I myself am good fortune.

Henceforth, I whimper no more, postpone no more, I need nothing.

I'm done with indoor complaints, libraries, and querulous criticisms.

Strong and content I travel the open road . . .

'After dinner (i.e. we set off at about half past four) we went towards Rydale for letters. It was a cold "Cauld Clash". The rain had been so cold that it hardly melted the snow. We stopped at Park's to get some straw in William's shoes. The young mother was sitting by a bright wood fire with her youngest child upon her lap and the other two sat on each side of the chimney. The light of the fire made them a beautiful sight, with their innocent countenances, their rosy cheeks and glossy curling hair. We sat and talked about poor Ellis, and our journey over the Hawes. It had been reported that we came over in the night. Willy told us of three men who were once lost in crossing that way in the night, they had carried a lantern with them—the lantern went out at the tarn and they all perished. Willy had seen their cloaks drying at the public house in Patterdale the day before their funeral. We walked on, very wet, through the clashy cold roads in bad spirits at the idea of having to go as far as Rydale, but before we had come again to the shore of the lake, we met out patient, bow-bent friend with his little wooden box at his back. "Where are you going?" said he. "To Rydale for letters." "I have two for you in my box." We lifted up the lid and there they lay. Poor fellow, he straddled and pushed on with all his might but we soon outstripped him far away when we had turned back with our letters. We were very thankful that we had not to go on, for we should have been sadly tired. In thinking of this I could not help comparing lots with him! He goes at that slow pace every morning, and after having wrought a hard day's work returns at night, however weary he may be, takes it all quietly, and though perhaps he neither feels thankfulness, nor pleasure when he eats his supper, and has no luxury to look forward to but falling asleep in bed, yet I daresay he neither murmurs nor thinks it hard.'

So runs Dorothy Wordsworth's diary entry for Monday morning, 8 February, 1802. It's a note that says everything about the huge difference between having to walk, as the postman had to each day with letters in a box on his back, and walking from choice to enjoy the stroll and the surroundings, as the Wordsworths did in their adoptive Lake District. It is often claimed that it was William Wordsworth and his sister Dorothy whose travels on foot and the writings associated with them—the poems, essays, dairies and letters—laid the foundations for walking as a romantic discipline. Before that, walking had been regarded as a necessity, you walked because your work or your situation demanded it, or because you were too poor to travel by horse or in a cart. Walking was associated with vagrancy and crime, poverty and want. The wretched roads were tramped by beggars and wanderers, by the poor and unemployed, by musicians and pedlars, by the homeless and by vagabonds, and none of them would dream of describing life on the road as an idyll, as a tour of enlightenment towards understanding and freedom. The Wordsworths understood this perfectly well. They understood poverty and always took it seriously; William was a rebel and revolutionary, writing hotly about social injustice and class divides, always with tenderness and compassion when in his poems he depicted the outcast and the poor. In the summer of 1790 he'd set out on foot for a long journey through Europe with his friend Robert Jones. They witnessed the outbreak of the French Revolution with which Wordsworth instantly sympathized. The following summer he seriously considered becoming a tramp and spending the rest of his life drifting. He never shook off his restlessness and poverty, they were his constant companions, even during the years when he was settled and famous. Of his sister, Dorothy Wordsworth, Virginia Woolf wrote: 'Through her parlour window Dorothy looked out and saw whoever might be passing—a tall beggar woman perhaps with her baby on her back; an old soldier; a coroneted landau with touring ladies peering inquisitively inside. The rich and the great she would let pass—they interested her no more than cathedrals or picture galleries or great cities; but she could never see a beggar at the door without asking him in and questioning him closely. Where had he been? What had he seen? How many children had he? She searched into the lives of the poor as if they held in them the same secret as the hills.' Dorothy Wordsworth's diaries are one of the great works of English literature; she investigated language and precision in the same way as she investigated poverty and nature, and she gradually developed a style whose observations and descriptions were so exact and so detailed that she became one of the great exponents of nature in her time; a time when English literature was being redefined by the friends Coleridge, Hazlitt, De Quincey and her brother William. With hindsight it seems that Hazlitt may have been right in his assessment of Coleridge; it wasn't only his gait that was vacillating, he didn't write directly enough either, and apart from certain individual poems, he isn't rated in the same class as William and Dorothy Wordsworth. Virginia Woolf wrote: 'They were uncertain of the way, and did not know where they would find lodging: all they knew was that there was a waterfall ahead. At last Coleridge could stand it no longer. He had rheumatism in the joints; the Irish jaunting car provided no shelter from the weather; his companions were silent and absorbed. He left them. But William and Dorothy tramped on. They looked like tramps themselves. Dorothy's cheeks were brown as a gipsy's, her clothes were shabby, her gait was rapid and ungainly. But still she was indefatigable; her eye never failed her; she noticed everything.'

An attempt

I am making notes in my diary: from the table by the window I can see out to the ferry quay and a small marina filled with pleasure craft; floating houses with little living rooms and lamps and television screens, you sit on your sofa as if you're always at home. You're on holiday; that comfortable living room moves from place to place invalidating the holiday itself; you leave nothing behind, arrive at nothing new. Apart from a few small waves, a bit of wind and rain, you float carelessly away, just as you would lying on your living room sofa, towards a place you've already arrived at: you're not travelling, you're sleeping.

The luxury boats, the cars, the over-large houses, they're growing, wealth is growing, but the people who inhabit them are getting smaller, they're almost invisible, they disappear among their own things. It almost seems as if this new wealth is invested in distancing ourselves from our surroundings. We lift ourselves over other people, insulate ourselves from natural things, shut out the foreign and the unknown, we conquer travel and buy ourselves out of unpleasantness and difficulty; everything that can provide new and unforeseen experience. It almost seems we're investing money in an entirely new form of idiocy.

The idiocy of new wealth. The idiocy of outsized summer cabins and houses. The idiocy of excessive numbers of cars. How many cars does a man need? How many rooms does a house need? How many toilets does a capitalist need? How much idiocy can a society endure? The idiocy of fast money. The idiocy of consumerism. The idiocy of greed. The idiocy of this new wealth.

From my table by the window I can see across to the long wooden bar with its beer taps and beer glasses hanging up in rows on the ceiling; the three backs leaning forward across the counter towards the figure walking up and down behind the bar. A girl in her twenties wearing a black blouse with a black apron tied in front of her light blue jeans. They like looking at her. I like looking at her, we like looking at her, she likes being looked at. The place fills up with young and old, billiards is being played in a side room; the clinking of glasses and billiard-balls like shots through the bar where bodies are elbowing round and nudging each other, in and out from the walls, until they fall out of the door. Outside, cigarettes are being smoked. The sound of voices, the smell of tobacco, glowing cigarettes, it gets dark, the sun goes down, leaving behind a soft, bluish light, Midsummer's Night. At midnight, there'll be a performance of Shakespeare's *A Midsummer Night's Dream* on the church green behind Askvoll Church, I've seen the flyer; local players, a new translation in the local dialect, ticket: one hundred kroner. Bring your own food and drink, a rug and something to sit on.

I'm waiting for a friend.

Order a bottle of wine. Sit at the table making notes. What's the point of walking? Why not drive a car, go by boat or train, why not fly, travel like other people, move like others; I love driving a car, getting behind the wheel, starting the engine and driving away, driving fast with the music on full volume and smoking cigarettes, window down, speed high; I like sitting on a train looking out of the window; seeing the landscape roll past while I tentatively read a novel: Vaksdal, Trengereid, Dale, Evanger, Voss, and the first snow, the first frost, the first kiss in the snow on the frozen stone wall down by the lake shore at Vangsvatnet; winter, summer, spring and the train rolls past; I love flying, sitting up in the air, sleeping up in the air and dreaming up in the air, I fall asleep and wake, eat breakfast up in the air, watch television and order wine with my meal, whisky with my coffee, gin with my dessert, and get drunk up in the air, lighter and freer up in the air; but most of all I like travelling by boat, going into the terminal on the quay and up the gangway to find my cabin in the bowels of the boat, the belly of the fish, lying in the depths and hearing the sounds of the engines and the sea, turning off the light and resting, sailing, sinking deeper into a larger stomach; night, mother, birth and death, I weep in the bottom of the boat.

Well, why walk when you can sail? Why walk when you can drive or fly? Why this slowness, this loneliness, all this exertion and stress, why this unnoticed rebellion, this unheard protest, this attempt to make something different and difficult? I have always wanted to live differently, in a manner quite at odds with the way I was brought up. From childhood a deep aversion to doing what I was told. I have always wanted to make things harder for myself. Never easier, never simpler, but ever more burdensome and always impossible for myself. And where has it got me? It hasn't got me anywhere normal; I've never had a job, haven't managed to get a home, a family, a regular income. I'm sitting in a borrowed house listening to Gypsy music; Fanfare Ciocarlia, Taraf de Haidouks, I heard them in Førde, at a folk music festival in Førde; ten Gypsies on the stage; accordion, cimbalom, fiddles, singing and pipes, faster and faster, round and round: without dresses there is no wedding, quicker and quicker as if the music wants to get our clothes off, off with jackets, off with shoes, off with dresses, dissolve the marriage, leave the job, sell the house and get out on the road, dance! I heard the music again in Romania, on a cassette in the rattling car as Narve and I drove out of Sighişoara with the two sisters who taught at the Gypsy village; trumpets and trombones, clarinet and horns, cornets and tubas, and it must have been the devil's music because we became crazed and mad, bawled and drank and sang in the back seat until the two Romanian sisters stopped the car and warned us of what awaited in the mahala where the tziganes lived. When you meet the

Gypsies, all romantic notions of Gypsies disappear. New ideas take shape, as imprecise and ethereal as the ones they replaced. What remains is the village—the flimsy, ramshackle houses, the muddy roads, that indescribable poverty in the heart of Europe—and the knowledge that it's impossible to live like the Gypsies, at least for me who'd imagined that we had something in common: a homelessness, a poverty, a sense of exile and isolation, but no, we are poor and homeless in completely different ways. We are excluded and alone for quite different reasons. We are different and we don't understand one another. A meeting requires time and frankness, patience and courage, and we had none of them, we came and went, drove downcast and silent out of the village and back to the house where we lived with the Romanian family. We felt at home there. Ashamed? Yes. In the big, two-storey house with rooms furnished with bookshelves and books, a double bed and our own television set, bathroom and patio, a wide staircase down to the living room and an open-plan kitchen where the women are preparing food, mother and grandmother, the two daughters, dressed up for a party, laughter and cigarettes, vodka and sweet white wine in a punch with fruit and lemon soda, the proud father with pomade in his hair, his expansive gesture of welcome and in we go, through the glass doors into the dining room with its long table laid for twelve; family and friends, food and drink, music and dance, a big party in our honour—we who are moving on. Ashamed? No. Ecstatic and tipsy, adventurous and grateful: wealthy Bohemians with Visa Cards and Norwegian passports, well-heeled layabouts, privileged travellers, on foot, dressed as wayfarers.

I'm sitting here waiting for a friend.

I'm sitting in the pub at Askvoll waiting for Narve Skaar. He's getting the bus from Førde, we'll take the boat to Bremanger tomorrow and stay on the beach at Grotler for a few days. The long, white sandy beach with crystal-clear water. We'll rest and swim, lie in the sun. We'll talk and argue as we always do. We'll lie on the sand and read as we always do. Watch the people passing through. We'll sleep on the beach, make a fire and drink wine and spirits as we always do. I'm looking forward to it. It's a moonlit night. Tonight they're performing Shakespeare's *A Midsummer Night's Dream*; it must be the beginning of a lengthy festival, of summer and fairytale? Or is it, as in the play within the play, the beginning of 'The most lamentable comedy and most cruel death of Pyramus and Thisby'?

A midsummer night's dream

A dream. What is a dream? I wake up from a dream, what was it I was dreaming? A few seconds ago I knew exactly what I dreamt, I told myself that it was something I must remember, and now it's all gone. I remember nothing of my dream. It seemed so concrete and substantial, as if it were real and important, but as soon as I woke up and opened my eyes, it evaporated and vanished. I've lost my dream. Like losing a key: I'm standing at the front door of the house where I'm living, I want to enter, I want to go home, but the key is missing, I can't find it. I'm locked out, outside the house I rent and am searching through my pockets; a credit card, some pills, loose change and no keys. For several minutes I'm homeless, what should I do? It's summer, the weather's mild, it's a moonlit night, I make up my mind to sleep out. I find a place in the garden, under the apple tree, make up a bed using twigs and my coat, pull my sweater over me like a duvet. Lie beneath the tree looking up at its branches and at the stars, hear the restless birds, aren't they asleep? Tomorrow she'll come with her key, the woman I live with. Now I remember my dream. I dreamt that you had left me, that I was alone, I was alone again.

'I have had a dream, past the wit of man to say what dream it was. Man is but an ass if he go about to expound this dream. Methought I was—there is no man can tell what. Methought I was, and methought I had, but man is but a patch'd fool, if he will offer to say what methought I had. The eye of man hath not heard, the ear of man hath not seen, man's hand is not able to taste, his tongue to conceive, nor his heart to report, what my dream was.'

This is Bottom's line just after he's fallen asleep and woken up right in the middle of the performance of: 'The most lamentable comedy and most cruel death of Pyramus and Thisby'. The comedy is a play within the play, a dream within the dream, a part of Shakespeare's *A Midsummer Night's Dream*. Narve and I half sit, half lie on the church green behind Askvoll church, surrounded by trees and spinneys, the moon is out, it's midnight and a Midsummer Night. I've never seen a better production. I've never laughed so loud and so long. We double up with laughter, the next moment there is a transformation, there's the sound of crying, a mother hushes, a father smokes, we can see and hear how the audience reacts to the performance they've become a part of.

QUINCE. Have you sent to Bottom's house? Is he come home yet?

STARVELING. He cannot be heard of. Out of doubt he is transported.

FLUTE. If he come not, then the play is marr'd; it goes not forward, doth it?

QUINCE. It is not possible. You have not a man in all Athens able to discharge Pyramus but he.

FLUTE. No; he hath simply the best wit of any hand-icraft man in Athens.

QUINCE. Yea, and the best person too; and he is a very paramour for a sweet voice.

FLUTE. You must say 'paragon'. A paramour is—God bless us!—a thing of naught.

NARVE. Now you see just how redundant institutional theatre is. Better to do plays in the open air. Or even better; get rid of art, get rid of lies and play-acting, and let life itself be drama.

TOMAS. Well, now I think you're overstating—or understating if you see the whole thing from higher up, where I'm lying, looking down on you. You're speaking beneath me and above yourself; surely you can't mean that we should get rid of art?

NARVE. Art is vanity and snobbery, and totally unnec-essary in life, at least if we're really living it.

TOMAS. We're lying here in the middle of a Shakespeare play, you're laughing and I'm crying, do you mean we're not living, that we're lying here half-dead and wholly dead and that we might as well bury art? I believe that we live life more intensely and intimately when we expose ourselves to art.

115

NARVE. This Shakespeare play is proof that the theatre is a joke. That's why I laugh and you cry, we
would both rather be running around the forest
being lovers ourselves, than sitting here watching
a play.

TOMAS. And yet it's Shakespeare who's getting us to
ponder this paradox; do we want to be onlookers
or participants, and do we stop participating when
we're challenged and mocked, when we look on
at our own foolishness?

NARVE. Master Shakespeare teaches us nothing. The
theatre doesn't make us better people. The theatre
is pure entertainment and pastime. And that's
what most of Shakespeare's plays tell us; that life
is too short and fleeting to waste it on misunder-
standings and plays.

BOTTOM. Masters, you ought to consider with yourself to bring in—God shield us!—a lion among
ladies is a most dreadful thing; for there is not a
more fearful wild-fowl than your lion living; and
we ought to look to't.

SNOUT. Therefore another prologue must tell he is not
a lion.

BOTTOM. Nay, you must name his name, and half his
face must be seen through the lion's neck; and he
himself must speak through, saying thus, or to the
same defect: 'Ladies,' or 'Fair ladies, I would wish

you' or 'I would request you' or 'I would entreat you not to fear, not to tremble. My life for yours! If you think I come hither as a lion, it were pity of my life. No, I am no such thing; I am a man as other men are'.

Sleeping out

I have always liked sleeping outside. Finding a spot high up or in a forest, or just outside the house, under a tree in the garden, or on the terrace when I'm visiting friends, spreading out the sleeping mat and crawling into my sleeping bag to spend the night under an open sky.

I sleep outside as often as I can, settle myself beneath a bush or tree, find a lean-to or a roof, a specially suitable place; a clearing in the forest, a view of the sea; here I'll lie thinking about how nice it is to sleep indoors, and that's the way I practise sleeping outside.

'I once knew a man who, as a matter of principle, would never sleep in his own house because, he said, his name was a name for people who wanted to sleep outside. This isn't a bitter recollection.'

So wrote Erik Satie. He characterized some of his own compositions as musical furnishings; they were to have functions equivalent to heating, lighting and ventilation. He got the idea from Matisse, who dreamt of an art without distracting elements, one that would be comparable to a good armchair. Satie spent most of his time away from his home, either with friends or in cafes. Or he would walk the streets. The reason for this was that the rooms he rented were miserable and cold. Satie loved wealth, but the small room at 6 Rue Cortot where he lived was plainly furnished. A fireplace, a mirror. A window ('I can see all the way to Belgium') and a bed. The bed was homemade. After only a few months in the little room, Satie was forced by poverty ('Poverty entered my room like a wretched little girl with great, green eyes') to move into an even smaller one. This room was so small that the bed prevented its only door from opening fully. Visitors had to squeeze in and clamber across the bed, one of them wrote that the room was so draughty and cold that Satie slept with his clothes and boots on. But by comparison with the man whose name meant that he had to sleep outside, Satie's existence was sumptuous and comfortable. My name is unconnected with anyone who wanted to sleep outside, all my family prefers to sleep inside, as they've done for generations, and I automatically assumed the habit until the night I slept outside for the first time. This was in Spain. A friend and I were travelling, a rail tour through Europe, we were seventeen or eighteen at the time. We'd journeyed a little distance on foot from San Sebastian, we wanted to walk along the north coast, but our packs were too heavy and we had to rest our legs, so in Santona Laredo we caught the train, only to hop quickly off again at the sight of that white bay which stood out somehow from the many little places the local train passed along the Bay of Biscay. The line curved and we caught a glimpse of the beach from the railway bridge. It was enough to make the pair of us react. The beach lay in a fold of the landscape, beneath the bridge a small river ran down the valley and out into the sea; the beach was partially concealed by woods and the surrounding hills; a small secret. We rose in unison, it was one of those moments when we were moved by something alien yet familiar; we exchanged a few quick words and got off the train at the next station. We walked back along the railway line, until we were stopped by the bridge; it spanned the valley and the river, we had to cross the bridge to get down to the beach. The bridge was single-track and narrow, roughly two hundred yards long, it was more than a hundred and fifty feet down to the river below. What were we to do? Erik put his ear to the rails. Could we hear a train far enough away to allow us to cross the bridge in safety? We waited for a train, so that we had some information to go by. But no train came. We decided to run across, jettison our packs if a train came, climb through the railings, hold on tight to the outside of the bridge and hope for the best. For a long time both of us listened to the rails. Nothing. Still nothing at all. Nothing at all, nothing at all, like an unheard rhythm, an invisible train. Then we began to run. We ran across the bridge. We didn't know which direction a train might come from, but we both saw and heard the train as we ran, it came from both directions, from everywhere; we saw it come through the air like a bird, we saw it sail towards us like breathing ship. But it was pure imagination and we ran through the air, flew across the bridge.

That day was a dream.

The beach was an extension of a military encampment. The bathers on the beach were soldiers and officers' families, sons and daughters, wives and children. We tore off our clothes, ran out into the waves, swimming and laughing. A soldiers' paradise. We ate at the little beach restaurant, sat in the shade beneath the leafy canopy, drank beer and ordered Spanish potato and onion omelettes. Three girls sat at the next table. They were sipping Coca Cola through straws. We asked them where we were. Don't you know where you are? No. They told us. But we can't speak to you, not now. Our fathers. Soldiers. She saluted, raising her hand to an invisible brim, sighted us with her straws and fired da-da-da-da-da as we closed our eyes and pretended to be dead. But I could see that she was only about sixteen, possibly seventeen, and it was hard to keep my eyes off her. But where are you staying? she asked in a low voice. We're going to sleep here on the beach. Like Gypsies, white Gypsies? Laughter. We'll be back, later, when it's dark.

We waited for darkness. Washed and shaved in the river. Clean shirts, a bottle of wine, each lying under his own tree, talking and smoking. Finally the sun went down. We lay listening for voices and footsteps, but we heard nothing except the waves and the wind that caressed the trees. The lights went out in the beach restaurant. A car started and lit up the road that threaded up the hillside. Then all was dark. It was a while before we could see the moon and the stars, they made small trails of light on the sand and the water where the waves flattened out and the sea turned calm.

They weren't coming.

We lay looking at the clouds. It was as if the natural things about us were withdrawing, were covering themselves in a blanket of darkness, we were deserted. Now I was waiting for night and for sleep. Did I sleep? I heard someone whistle. And there they were, the three girls, followed by a small group carrying a pail, a tin pail filled with wine and pop. The girl called Teresa came first, dressed in a short skirt and wearing high-heels, with make-up on, she seemed older than she had earlier in the day. There you are! she called. We've brought along some friends, for protection, they soldiers da-da-da-da-da, she said.

We built a fire on the beach. One of the boys had brought along a guitar, he sang and imitated a trumpet by making whistling sounds through a plastic funnel. We clapped to the rhythm and danced with each of the girls, but I tried to keep hold of the one called Teresa. My name is Teresa Torras, she said. She was tall and dark with long hair tied in a pony tail. Major Torras is my father, she said. She had lovely, pale breasts which could be seen under her blouse. Anna Torras is my mother. We danced and I didn't

want to let go of her. I held her, it was like holding someone you never want to let go of. I said to her: I'm not going
to let go of you. She laughed and tried to draw away.
Antonio Torras is my brother, she said. And this time she
nodded to the boy who was playing the guitar, he followed
us with his eyes. She tried to wriggle free, but I held her
firmly. I'm not letting go of you, I said. They called to us
from the fire. I knew that as soon as I let her go she'd be
lost. I want to see you again tomorrow, I said. She nodded.
I knew I wouldn't see her again. We sat down with the
others, I released her, but she kept close to me. My name is
Tomas Torras, I said. My joy was short-lived. But long
enough that I can still see her: that beautiful, brazen face,
the serious eyes, the tall, wayward body; I'm holding her
and won't let her go.

During the night it began to rain. Erik slept wearing
earplugs, it was a habit of his. I couldn't sleep. In my mind's
eye I'd got Teresa Torras out of her blouse and her skirt. She
was naked. I felt the rain against my face. An ardent, wet
tongue. I'd end up soaked, opened my sleeping bag, turned
to Erik, shook his shoulder. He woke up. Pulled one earplug
out. Irritated. What is it? he growled. It's started raining, I
said. Well, what are you going to do about it? he said, turned
away and slept on. Well, what was I going to do about it? I
had to smile. It was raining and there was nothing I could do
about it. I lay awake. Listened to the rain beating on the
leaves, it wrested a sweet, mouth-like smell of moisture from

the woods; it emanated from the earth and the darkness, opening up and I thrust in and gave way, the spasm went through my body, a squirt of warmth that spurted out in all the wetness.

On the beach

Narve and I have decided to take the express boat to Bremangerlandet, walk out to the beach at Grotler and sleep out there. A few days and nights on the beach, until the weather breaks, then the idea is to head north, as far as we can go, we've got the entire summer.

We buy what we need at Askvoll: toiletries, plaster for blisters, bottles of water and painkillers, sleeping pills, sedatives, a small pharmacy, in addition to what Narve has bought from the off-licence at Førde: two wine boxes and two bottles of spirits, we divide the load between our packs. A torch, sunglasses, two penknives, good and sharp, a Thermos and four Hamsun paperbacks which Narve has purchased for the trip. Neither of us has been up as far as Nordland. We joke about walking all the way there; the route August travelled in *Wayfarers*, but in reverse, Hamsun wrote that August was away for several months, but then took a boat back to Pollen. Narve is wearing light mountain boots and has a complete set of Gore-Tex equipment; blue windproof jacket, white shirt and yellow, waterproof polyester trousers that glow. They're the most hilarious trousers I've ever seen, and I've seen them many times, in many places, he always wears them. Up mountains and in towns, at bars and restaurants; they're wonderful and vital trousers, because it's impossible to be in a bad mood when you're walking behind or next to such trousers. I'm dressed in a suit and Doc Martens boots. It's a constant satisfaction to meet other hikers, on mountain top or plateau, in valleys or uplands, wearing a shirt and suit.

We sit at the front of the boat, eating prawn sandwiches and drinking coffee, looking out of the front window: at the places we pass, the jetties, the shops, the people waiting. These fair, tough, patient faces. This difficult land. Mountainous and steep, small farms, small places, the big distances. The arduous work. Animals and man, trees and isolated fields, boathouses and boats. A beautiful land. The sun is shining, it's a lovely day. The sea is calm, smooth, like a road stretching out, we're motionless, speeding along the coast.

We're living in the best of all worlds, I say. In the best of all times. I wouldn't want to live in any other place, in any other time. Our country's become rich, and we are the richest of all, we've freed ourselves from work, I say, from responsibility, from toil, from our families, from shame. We're free and rich, and I'm not ashamed.

Don't you miss it?

Miss what?

What we've torn ourselves free from.

No.

We go ashore at Bremanger. Set out for Grotler. For the beach. It's hot, we walk on the road, noticing the gardens and houses, garages and cars, the new riches.

We've got richer and our buildings have got worse, says Narve. These new houses, they're not good enough, too ugly; flimsy, rectangular boxes encumbered with patios and external decoration, they look dreadful. We've got richer and live worse, that's what it seems like. Everything looks worse: houses, schools, filling stations, post offices and supermarkets. We've got richer and we build more crudely, we've become stingy, stingy with life, our lives are wretched and impoverished, in spite of the wealth, it has made us poor in a new way, a worse way. We look worse. Too fat, too lethargic, too tired, our muscles are out of condition, our bodies are disintegrating. And our faces. We've become fatter and slower and look stupider. Our clothes are homogeneous and standardized, we dress the way we live, conforming to poor taste. We watch too much television and read too many newspapers and allow ourselves to be influenced by too much inanity. It really does seem that way. Take a look around! We mock beauty. We disturb nature, destroy the landscape. We torture animals and ruin things for ourselves. We've become rich at the expense of something and someone, and that worries me. I feel ashamed.

I see.

It's a sense of shame that binds us to others, that makes us part of what we see, says Narve. We can't imagine ourselves independent of what we see, of others, it's a sense of shame that makes us human and partly responsible, its impossible to do anything about a sense of shame.

I see.

My good spirits are steadily evaporating. The sun is high in the sky and things look black. No clouds, no breeze, just the long, black ribbon of asphalt that winds between appalling houses and factory-like barns in which animals are imprisoned so they don't lose weight, or to produce more eggs; or is the silence the result of the farmer's indolence, his laziness? Where is he? Where are the people, where are the animals? Where are the men cutting grass and the women drying the hay on racks and the kids jumping in it? Where are the cattle grazing, the hens kicking, the cock crowing and the goats bleating, where are the sheep and the pigs, where are the horses and the dogs? Well, what has happened to agriculture in the Norwegian landscape?

It lies there quiet and confined, almost forsaken on a hilltop, farm after farm, many of them deserted and overgrown with bushes and scrub, thistles and weeds. Tumbledown houses and empty barns, a depressing sight, for we are witnessing something that is in the process of vanishing: agriculture in western Norway.

This makes me think of the nostalgia evoked by derelict factories and industrial communities, that strident nostalgia of the novel and the book, of the newspaper article and the interview; why isn't there any for the most far-reaching change in our country's modern history: the abandonment of Norwegian farming?

The death of Norwegian agriculture is occurring simultaneously with an even greater destruction of the Norwegian countryside. The Norwegian landscape is threatened on two fronts, from nature and from culture, it is healing, it is being reconstructed. We're building in precisely the same way in the country as we build in the cities, and our first glimpse of a rural community is like the first glimpse of any suburb: a petrol station, a shopping centre. American villas, satellite dishes. Presumably television has taught us how homes should be built. Big garages, new gardens, patios and barbecues; the Norwegian-American family, standing in the garden grilling, disguised as Norwegians. American immigration is greater than Norwegian emigration to the US. But the Americans have arrived in a somewhat unusual way, they have ridden and driven, sailed and flown, shot and broken their way into Norwegian homes, into Norwegian living rooms, right out of the television screen and into Norwegian daily life.

The first thing we come to on the road to Grotler is a shopping centre. Post office, supermarket, a large car park. We buy a few cans of beer and a packet of cigarettes, sit down at the table next to the car park, tired and thirsty, hot and silent, the sun is baking, I recognize the smell of salt and sea. The white light, the screaming gulls. And suddenly, two girls walk past, it's summer, we're at the beach.

A ray of happiness; we have no plans, nothing to do. We're going to lie on the beach.

We walk the last mile or two out to Grotler sands; the houses get smaller, older, they've been here a long time. Suffered wind and weather, extensions and additions, influx and tourism. The houses are simple and weatherproof, they stand there as if fixed to the ground with invisible bolts, white and yellow, they have taken on the colours of the beach, sand-yellow, ochre-white, light blue: a green door. A window with red curtains; it's the same shade as the underside of a wet stone, or the mark on a gull's bill, or current-riffled eelgrass. The houses stand in a row facing the sea, one side to the ocean, the other to the narrow road; up beneath the mountain ridge that stretches out like a tongue towards the sea, are the old hay-sheds bereft of all traces of paint and tar, grey as rocks, or like the trees they've begun to resemble, split and colourless. And then; between the houses and the trees, round a small bend past the boathouses and sea rocks, is the beach. Grotler sands. A long, white arc, or a bowl filled with sea; the water pours in and spills out in a never-ceasing motion, apart from a few quiet hours in the middle of the night when the sea seems frozen by moonlight. And in the middle of the day, the sun is high in the sky; the sea sleeps. Windless. The tall grasses that grow along the margin between the enclosed fields and the sand, stand still. We walk along the beach, right out to the sea rocks where the beach ends, here is a depression and two rocks which give natural cover from the rest of the long beach; it's our spot for relaxing. We toss off our packs, and our clothes, run towards the water's edge and throw ourselves in. The water is cold. The sea is cold and hard, like a skin, we dive and swim over the sandy bottom, out towards the deep and up again towards the water's edge, now we feel the heat. The heat from the sun and the salt, we float. We swim out to the little bird island, clamber up, lie on the flat rocks and look back at the beach.

Have you ever seen such a lovely sight?

No.

The beach with the mountain behind, the grass and the fences that climb the fell side. The houses in a row, the gardens and trees, the narrow road that runs down to the beach, and spread out on the sand, as if silence and sleep has attacked all living things like a gas, the bathers, lying on the beach. On towels and blankets, between baskets and plastic bags, mattresses and parasols, the pale bodies, bloated with heat and sleep. A dog capers at the water's edge. The birds fly up, a mother calls to a child which has fallen and the silence is broken. A man dives, a car starts and the engine drives life into all that has slept, the beach reawakens, assumes its normal routine and customary movements; they play ball and run, bathe and swim.

The hottest hour of the day is past.

The day turns. A gentle onshore breeze, ripples and waves, a cloud covering the sun, we swim back to land, lie on the sand; this is the perfect day. We lie in the sun, sleep in the sun, do nothing, want nothing, dream. What are we dreaming about? I'm dreaming about a new life on the road, always on the move, on foot from place to place. Is it possible? It is possible. How long? I don't know. In the autumn we'll head south, in the winter even further south, to North Africa and down towards the warmth, always towards the warmth. How far can you go? I don't know. I still haven't tried to test my own limits, I've always walked with a goal and a time plan. I've always gone on trips, short or long, but never longer than I originally planned. Two months. Even three months, but then I went home, by train or bus, plane or boat. But just now at this point in my life I haven't got a home. I've got a place to live, I live alone, a room with a mattress on the floor, a writing table, a chair, that's all. A waiting room. I'm waiting for a change, no, I'm waiting for a metamorphosis, something quite new, a new life? What am I waiting for? This new life begins today, these new possibilities, I only have to rise, stand up and shake off the sand and the dream, put on my suit and hoist my pack on my back, walk away, down the open road.

PART 2

Sport and entertainment

I've always enjoyed walking. One day, it was in spring, I went out for a stroll; on my way out of town I saw a car, it was parked under a tree, a yellow Mercedes with red leather seats. A piece of cardboard was stuck to the side window: for sale, it said, and underneath was a phone number. I rang the number and bought the car, it's the most magnificent car I've ever owned. The day after I bought the Mercedes I drove across the mountains to Oslo, spent the night at a guest house, drove on to Copenhagen and slept on the back seat of the car, before driving on down through Germany and into Holland and through Belgium and across the border into France where I stopped and parked the car in Charleville-Mézières. From Charleville I continued on foot—first along the River Meuse, then by the side of the Canal des Ardennes to Le Chesne, and up the River Aisne to Vouziers, through forests and across fields on dusty paths— towards Reims and Paris. It took me five days, I trudged into the big city one Friday, tired and dirty; I'd been sleeping rough. I entered the city through the Porte de Clignancourt, collided with the streets and the throng of people: a sudden wall of noise and city. I went through the city gate and was blinded by the light, the city light; a

135

confusion of faces and hands, eyes and houses, windows and streets, of doors and possibilities; where should I go? I sat down and put my hands to my face. For a minute or two. Then I ordered a drink, but they wouldn't serve me, the waiter waved at me and pushed me away. In my hotel room I looked at myself in the mirror, I looked like a down-and-out. A tramp, unshaven, a tear in the jacket of my suit, muddy trousers up to my knees. I stood in front of the wardrobe mirror and was satisfied. This was the way I'd always wanted to look. I lit a cigarette, opened a plastic bottle of wine and lay down on the bed. At last I was content, at last I'd arrived: I'd become someone else.

I spent two days in bed. Breakfast was left on a tray outside my door; coffee, a croissant, some bread and marmalade. It was nine o'clock, the church bells rang, the sunlight came through the window and went round the room as if it was at home there; I ate breakfast in bed. The chair, the writing table, the mirror, the wardrobe, the carpet, all this belonged to the room; the furniture had its home and belonged there, I was the stranger. I lay in bed reading Rilke's *Letters on Cézanne*. I found great pleasure lying in bed and looking across at the window which was open. The window didn't belong to me, neither did the view or the sounds that filled the room; voices, footsteps, the street light at night, nothing of this was mine, it belonged to the room. I was content to lie in bed and look at the window, it was like a picture on the wall. I didn't want to see

Cézanne's paintings, it was enough to read Rilke; I could imagine the paintings: the kitchen table with apples and a bottle of wine, the portrait of the woman in the red armchair. 'In this red armchair, which has a personality,' Rilke wrote, it got me thinking about how fond I am of objects, of chairs and tables, beds and lamps, perhaps that's because I'm alone so much, at times objects are all I have to relate to. What was I doing in Paris? Nothing. I wanted to wander the streets. I wanted to hang about. I wanted to lie in bed. I wanted to sit on the windowsill of my hotel room and look down into the street at the people passing by. I had no greater plans. Yes, I had, I wanted to make some notes. One morning I took a train on the commuter line out to Arcueil-Cachan, where Erik Satie had had his home in a small room at 22 Rue Cauchy. Each day Satie walked from this address to the cafe that was his regular haunt in Paris, a walk of more than seven miles, interrupted only by the composer's many halts at his watering holes along the route, he was drunk by the time he finally arrived at the place where he was going to drink. There were evenings when he walked the whole way back, too, skint, full of ideas; it's said that he made regular stops under lamp posts to scribble down the notes he heard in a notebook. In conversation with John Cage, Roger Shattuck develops the theory that the source of Satie's appreciation of musical rhythms, the possibility of variation within repetition, the effect of boredom within the whole, could be this perpetual walking to and fro in the same landscape, day after day. I wanted to walk the same route, simply to make notes, nothing else: I wanted to write a book about walking, it was a good idea, the truth was that it didn't interest me any more. I took the train out of the city. Got off when the map told me I'd arrived; at the station there was a bar, I went in, it was a good beginning. Two men were propping up the counter, I stood next to them and lit a cigarette. I asked for an ashtray, but was told to drop my ash on the floor. Ashtrays are for putting money in, said the proprietor. I put two francs in the ashtray and chucked my cigarette end on the floor. You understand our French ways, said the proprietor. You want another drink? No thanks, I said. You have understood nothing, he said. I explained that I was looking for the house where Erik Satie lived, and immediately the man next to me wanted to drive me there, he wasn't sober: 'The house with the four chimneys,' he said; get into the car. The car was a dented, metal-grey Range Rover; we could have driven out of the city, out of France, down through Spain, taken the ferry to Morocco and driven into the desert. We could have driven far. We could have driven away. But the driver was drunk, he drove slowly and carefully to the street with the derelict house. It resembled the man who'd lived there. Eric Satie was an alcoholic, poor; the room he lived in was so small that the bed prevented the door from opening properly, but people didn't open it, Satie didn't have visitors, only once or twice, very few friends had seen the room where he slept for the last twenty-seven years of his life. This was the house. I sat in the front seat of the car, wound down the window, and I don't know why, but suddenly I had tears in my eyes, I turned away, perhaps I recognized the poverty, perhaps I recognized the loneliness, perhaps it was just the alcohol, I was out of kilter; what on earth was I doing here? What did I want here? Now you've seen it, the house, said my driver, what do you want to do? Where do you want to go? Back to Paris, I said. OK, we'll drive back. But now I had to protest. My idea is to walk into the city, on foot like Satie, I said. That's a bad idea, said the driver, he wanted to drive, presumably he wanted other things as well. Thanks for the lift, I said, what do I owe you? Sixty-three francs, he said with a professional air; that's exactly the price of three shots, I need to drink, he said. You could always sell your car, I said, it was meant as a joke, but he took it badly. Get out of the car, he shouted angrily, it struck me suddenly that he lived in that car; I'd just suggested that he sell his combined livelihood and home.

I began to walk into Paris. Africans in the streets, colourful dresses, a djellaba, my favourite costume; the way you disappear in clothes, become someone else, transmogrify. African youths in American clothes, jeans, hooded jackets, baseball caps and shoes, they hung about the streets, gathered at street corners, sat in cars; idleness, dissatisfaction, music, aggression. Hate. Riots. Revolution? I went into a bar, Le Fleuri, run by a Berber, every

Wednesday and Thursday they served Couscous Berber. The Berbers were playing a game of dice, winnings were paid out in drinks tokens. They drank. Cigarette stubs were thrown on the floor in front of the bar. I drank. I forgot Erik Satie, the Paris he walked in and belonged to no longer existed. North African faces, a smell of the south, a smell of poverty and disaffection, a sense of stagnation and boondocks; these desiccated lawns and tower blocks with rubbish-filled backyards where envy and hate grew. Pollution and noise, what had I expected? Grassy meadows? Fields and horses, tranquillity and idyll? Contemporary music had long since caught the pace and the din, the big city and the traffic, I was living in a time-warp, in a city which didn't exist, I was following a certain Monsieur Satie, a ghost in a brown velvet suit with a skullcap on his head. I was a ludicrous figure. Dressed in a suit and a white shirt with blood on my collar and shirt front. I had a nosebleed. Caused by all the exhaust. I was wearing worn-out shoes and filthy trousers, a leather bag on my shoulder. Inside the bag: a pen and my notebooks. What should I note down? That the leaves were coming out on the trees? That there were flowers in a window on the Rue de la Convention? That there was a couple sitting on a bench in the Jardin Duranton? That the suburbs would soon explode in riots and violence? It made me think of Des Esseintes in Huysmans' novel, *Against the Grain*; he suddenly wanted to go to London but only needed to travel a few blocks before he found a restaurant that reminded him of foreign places and England. So Esseintes was able to return home, happy after his successful journey to England.

After only half an hour I'd left Africa behind. Now I was walking through a French arrondissement, I'd crossed an invisible line, although the transition was noticeable, quieter streets, paler faces, darker clothes; suits and ties. A business district. Offices of Citroën and Peugeot, Mercedes and Ford. Hotels, the first metro station. A bridge, I walked across the Seine, past a football field, the players black, the referee white. I walked into Paris. The city was warm as a heart. Balzac wrote that Paris was the world's head, but the city was head and heart, feet and hands, stomach and breast, breath and lungs, a face, a mouth. I walked past the Terminus Hotel, down Avenue du Général Leclercq. The general didn't ring any bells with me, but the name Leclercq brought to mind the painter Balthus' maid, eighteen-year-old Lena Leclercq who had been recommended by Giacometti, she wanted to be a poet, but was exploited by Balthus, he used her as a model, misused her as domestic and lover, before replacing her with a younger girl; fourteen-year-old Frédérique, the daughter of his brother Pierre Klossowski. Lena Leclercq tried to commit suicide, was saved, moved to a remote farm in the mountains where she kept bees, planted a garden and produced a collection of poems, *Pomme endormie*. In 1983 I went to Paris alone to see a retrospective exhibition of Balthus' paintings at the

Pompidou Centre, it was a marvellous experience, one of the best I've had in terms of art. But what did I learn back then as a twenty-two year old, other than that the greatest works of art are created by people without moral scruples? At thirty-nine I should have known better, but still I walked down Avenue du Général Leclercq and wanted to travel back in time: I wanted to do something that wasn't me any more.

As I walked up Rue d'Amsterdam something peculiar occurred. Someone shouted my name. I walked on as if nothing had happened, but my name was called again, it wasn't my imagination. I halted, it was unpleasant, like being arrested, just before you start committing a crime. I was almost at my goal, what was I about to do? Wasn't I disguised in a foreign city, unknown to everyone? Didn't I have hidden aims, secret plans, plans that belonged to another: he who walked free and unknown in the streets of Paris? Who was it who'd unmasked me? I turned and found one of the cultural correspondents of Bergens Tidende, he was attending a seminar with some colleagues, but what was I doing here? Well, what could I say? Nothing, I could have said, nothing, is what I should have said, I'm making notes for a book, I told Frode Bjerkestrand. That made everything easier, we chatted for a few minutes, then I walked on. But something had changed. Something was ruined, I was no longer a stranger. I was no longer someone else, I'd been caught up with, in those few minutes I'd become myself.

And so it was me and no one else who walked through that door in Rue Jean Baptiste. A door of smoked glass, just before Place Pigalle, the bar was called Star, and up at the counter sat two girls. A black woman in a tight-fitting, light-green nearly-see-through top, her legs crossed, a black leather skirt and boots that reached to her knees, she was drinking Coke through a straw. The other was a girl from Eastern Europe, the Ukraine as it turned out, she said her name was Vivianne. She wasn't what I imagined a prostitute to be like, lightly made-up, short hair, a boyish face, beautiful. She appeared natural, normal, except for her clothing; a fur coat, half open, I could see she was naked underneath. She exposed herself. White breasts, pale skin. Then she did up the coat again, a small exhibition with her fingers. I'd seen her, now she was buttoning up, and it was in that instant that I began to want her. There was music, we talked. She told her story. About how she arrived in Paris from Kiev to dance, ballet, she said, but she'd lost her job, didn't get another one, and now she was working here, temporarily, she said, while she waited. And you? she asked, why are you here, haven't you got a girl?

Yes, I said, I have. I've got a girl.

She lowered her gaze, as I had done when she'd buttoned up her fur coat. We recognized one another, sat in the bar, talking and lying. It was only a matter of time before we'd go together, I liked this certainty; it scared me. Other guests arrived, there were more girls further in the locale, they got up in turn, as if in response to an unheard command; a shadow play, voices and smoke, women and men.

What's your name? I asked. She hesitated before replying, as if considering whether to tell the truth, or give the usual name, the business name.

You can call me what you like.

My name is Vivianne.

Have you done this before? she asked.

I shook my head.

It will end up costing quite a lot. First you must pay for what I drink and what you drink, and then for going upstairs with me, and then there are all the extras, the room and the sheets, towels and cleaning the coat, they come up with everything, she said, have you got enough money? she asked.

I nodded.

And then I must rip you off, she said. If you want me lying down it will cost a hundred francs extra. If you want me completely naked, if you want me to take my fur off, it will be a hundred francs extra. If you don't want to use a condom, it will be a hundred francs extra. You understand?

No, I said. What do the regulars do?

They agree a fixed price, in advance. They say what they want, this and this, in minute detail, and then you negotiate a price. They get just what they pay for, no more and perhaps less, the quickest is a blow-job, that's fast and it's the simplest, you feel cheated.

Why are you telling me this?

She shrugged her shoulders.

I've got a better suggestion, she said. Tomorrow's my day off, I'd like to do some completely normal things.

Normal things?

Eat at a restaurant, go to the cinema, do some window shopping. I'm alone, she said. Not exactly lonely, but alone.

But, I said.

Now I'm going to say my price out loud, she said. I'll tell you what I cost. And you've got to shake your head, you haven't got that sort of money, you'll object, and I'll get angry, and so will the staff. You'll have to pay through the nose for what we've drunk, I'll leave you in the bar, I've written my phone number on your matchbox, so please don't lose it or throw it away, and ring me in the morning.

But, I said. I really want you, right now, right here, I've got the money, I can pay.

I could see she was disappointed. She looked down, as if I'd failed her.

I cost two thousand francs, she said loudly. That's my price, nothing more and nothing less.

I shook my head in despair; it's too much, much too much, I said it loudly, and she got furious and left me in the bar.

Giacometti and the prostitutes

At 46 Rue Hippolyte-Maindron there was a studio. Jean
Genet described it as grey, and the man who lived there as
grey as the concrete walls of the studio. Alberto Giacometti
was said to be grey and dusty, constantly covered with clay
and paint, he worked in a grey suit, always wore a tie, even
when he was sitting in front of one of the sculptures which
he obviously regarded with the same reverence as the
women who'd stood as models for them. His studio was
much visited, Giacometti left it frequently, usually at night,
he would go to a restaurant or a nightclub, or to a brothel.
He didn't change, it was the artist on his way out, and his
garb announced that there was no difference between life
and work, daily life and work, art and work, everything was
work, even visits to a brothel. The artist's work included
everything; the morning shave and knotting his tie, the
hours in front of the easel and the hours with models and
sculpting, visits, conversations, the hours at the café and
the strolls there and back, the walks in the city and the
dinners with wine and cigarettes, that endless smoking, all
this was a part of Giacometti's ceaseless toil. Never resting,
he made love and smoked, dreamt and wrote, drew and
painted, talked and listened, saw and noted, he worked.

This was the workman who was so hugely attractive to certain women, perhaps because he loved women, because he so obviously worshipped them, perhaps also because he had something, a radiance, something that is lost in the photographs we see of him. When we look at the photographs Henri Cartier-Bresson took of Giacometti, perhaps they surprise us, he was hardly good-looking, and as grey as people said. He resembled one of his sculptures, nervous, thin, a large head. Perhaps Giacometti had taken shape from his own work. Moulding himself in his own image. Giacometti's was an extreme case; it's not possible to say whether the busts of his brother Diego have borrowed lines from a self-portrait, or if it's Giacometti who's taken features from the busts of his brother. In any case, immediately you see the busts, you think of Alberto Giacometti.

He contemplates one of his own sculptures.

HE. It's a bit bizarre, isn't it?

It's a word Giacometti often uses. He's a bit bizarre himself. He scratches his tousled grey head. Annette cut his hair. He hoists his grey trousers which have sagged over his shoes.

HE. When I'm out in the street and catch sight of a fully dressed whore, what I see is a whore. But back in my room, when she stands there naked before me, I see a goddess.

I. For me, a naked woman is simply a woman without clothes on. It doesn't touch me. I certainly don't see her as a goddess. But I see your sculptures the way you see naked prostitutes.

HE. Do you think I manage to show them as I see them?

Jean Genet, who wasn't transported at the sight of a naked woman, but who did see the divine in Giacometti's sculptures, adds, 'that if you placed the sculptures in a room, that room would become a temple'. Divine is a word often used to describe Giacometti's sculptures of women, but many of them were simply portraits of women he saw in brothels. Giacometti liked going to brothels, he went regularly, even after he was married, it didn't alter any of his habits. He worked from early to late, at night he went out, in the morning he'd come home, back to the studio in a taxi, alone or with a prostitute. He slept until two o'clock, ate and resumed his work. He made sculptures of men who were walking, on their way perhaps to the brothel where the women stood elevated on their plinths, as they are in Giacometti's female figures. Men who walk, women who stand. They stand on street corners or in front of a door; as impassive as his beloved mother, she who was on the other side of the door, inside the house, inside the home which she rarely left, the waiting woman that Giacometti identified with love and security all his life. Her name was Annetta Giacometti. Alberto's wife was called Annette Giacometti, it isn't merely the similarity of name that's striking, but also the close proximity between mother and wife: Giacometti placed them securely next to one another on the periphery of his art, in the centre stood the prostitutes, the women Giacometti went to as often as he could. Jacques Dupin, poet and friend of Giacometti, wrote: 'He missed the old bordellos. I believe they played such a big part in his life—and the memory of them still does—that one ought to mention them. He seems to have endowed them with an almost divine importance. He went there to fall on his knees to a cruel and goddess-like creature. The distance that his sculptures always create from the viewer, also perhaps existed between him and the naked whore. Each sculpture seems to be harkening back to—or emerging from—a night so distant and deep that it has become one with death; in the same way as the whore returns to the mysterious night over which she once reigned. And over on the shore he stands watching her getting smaller, and at the same time more impressive. And then, I wonder if brothels aren't precisely the places where woman can display a wound that never liberates her from her loneliness, and isn't it in the bordello that she's freed from all her useful attributes and thus in a way achieves a kind of purity?'

Today Giacometti would probably be labelled a whoremonger. More often he's called a great artist, and he was a great artist, what was distasteful and disquieting was that he created his great art from experiences we would describe as immoral acts. But in the Paris of the twenties and thirties it wasn't uncommon to visit brothels, they were regarded as exotic nightclubs. Simone de Beauvoir describes the most famous of them, Giacometti's favourite, Le Sphinx in her memoirs: 'One evening after the café closed the whole gang of us went to Le Sphinx, and I went too. Because of Toulouse-Lautrec and van Gogh I'd imagined bordellos as highly poetic places, and I wasn't disappointed. Furnishings, more flagrantly tasteless than the interior of Sacré-Coeur, glowing, half-naked women in their roomy, multi-coloured tunics—it was much better than the ridiculous paintings and fair stalls Rimbaud liked so much.' The comparison of the inside of the famous church with that of the brothel is striking, it put me in mind of Georges Bataille who wrote, in *Le Coupable*: 'My true church is a brothel; it is the only one that provides a sufficient lack of relief.' Lust is not to be assuaged, it should be investigated and described, it should be turned into art. 'I've long wished to write about this and certain other recollections about excretion and masturbation, but it wouldn't run to a whole book,' Giacometti said in his diaries. 'And also about all my nocturnal ramblings in 1923–24, when I scoured Paris for a prostitute. I seemed to be obsessed by prostitutes. No other women existed, only those who worked on the streets attracted and astonished me. I wanted to see them all, know them all, and every single night I'd begin my long, lonely strolls.' Giacometti liked walking, he loitered about the streets of Paris, sketching and making notes. It's almost as if the walking man is a kind of archetype for Giacometti; an original image or model: to be in motion, the figure stepping out and swinging his arms, where is he off to? What does he see? We recognize the figure, we're off to other places, to see other things, but Giacometti's sculptures have clarified and amplified two fundamental states of nature and man: to be in motion, and to be at rest.

I walked about Paris, selected and followed streets at random, walked without any aim or object, walked for walking's sake, to see; on the corner at the top of Boulevard du Montparnasse was a beggar, dressed in a white shirt and suit, a man in his late thirties, unshaven and with short hair. I got such a shock and had to stop, he had my face. I stood there, unable to walk on; he was holding out a paper cup at chest height, not meek and imploring, but demanding and with almost truculent dignity; no money was being put in the paper cup. I trembled with agitation. Should I go over and put money in the paper cup? Did I feel sorry for myself? I stood still. A cigarette. One step forward, one back; I wanted to know nothing about this man, tore myself away and followed a passer-by, she was wearing high heels and a short skirt, a folder under her arm, and after only a few hundred yards she was stopped by an unknown man, he asked some question or other and they stood there, a meeting, I crossed the road and could see him giving her his card; it made me anxious. I went into the nearest large shop, FNAC, a large bookstore; on the first floor there was an exhibition of photographs: black-and-white photos of Marguerite Duras' flats and houses: her spaces. 'It's inside a house that one is alone. Not outside, but inside it. In the garden there are birds, cats. And also sometimes a squirrel, a polecat. One isn't alone in a garden. But in a house one is so alone that one completely vanishes.' Marguerite Duras' loneliness. Populated by friends and lovers, by books and lamps, tables and chairs, mirrors and carpets, a telephone, it was in the middle of the writing table next to a whisky bottle beneath a lamp and amongst piles of papers. The work table. The desk, an ashtray, a packet of cigarettes, you could see they were Gitanes, but no author. She was absent in every photo. And yet was she there, the writer, in each and every room, in the house, unseen? Gone? Dead? She was absent, but present in all the things she surrounded herself with. I bought two books: *Ecrire* and *C'est tout*. Stuffed the books into my suit pocket and went back out into the streets, strolled down the boulevard, wanting to find a place to sit down, I wanted to write a letter. Sat for half an hour at a pavement cafe, couldn't concentrate, so much to see, so many people walking past, past. I went to the nearest metro station where I took the line to Poissonnière and ambled down to my hotel in the Rue Mazarin. Hôtel de Lille; I've stayed there at that hotel, every time I've come to Paris alone, Room 6, on the second floor, on the corner of the building with a view down to a cross-roads and the bar with the large window which gave me a view of the drinkers. The view was a reprise of the one I'd had as a child: from the living room window in Vestre Torggate I could look down at the windows of the guest house; the lamps and tables, the glasses and people, like the characters in a shadow play, a puppet theatre where an invisible father pulled the strings and made the hands rise on command: drink, smoke, hit, be a man, my boy. I pulled back the curtains, opened the windows of the hotel room and placed my chair in the aperture, in the front row, you might say, an onlooker at this puppet show, I would say: the nightly show based on *The Tales of Hoffmann* with music by Offenbach, bars from a march in a soldier carnival; an argument about a letter, concerning the love for a woman, or was it a puppet, a marionette, a prostitute? They worshipped an automaton, glorified work, art, it ended up as a love machine, they produced war and false notions, they produced repetitions; the same movements each evening, the same words, the same show every evening: theatre. Puppets. Alcohol. Glug! Glug! Glug! Glug! *Je suis la bière.* Glug! Glug! Glug! Glug! *Je suis le vin.* My vapour silvers the glasses! Ah! I gild them with divine fluid! Ah! Glug! Glug! Glug! We are mankind's friends. We chase away boredom and sorrow. Glug! Glug! Ah! From my window I could see the counter and the top of the woman's body standing behind it, her head was missing. The figures at the tables by the window had no legs. I couldn't hear the music, the voices of the place. Should I go down, go out, down the stairs and out of the door, cross the street and go in, in through the door and find the faces, the hands, the feet, the voices? Try to piece them together into a whole, a reality, a body? No. I'd sit here in the window and watch. This evening and every evening in this hotel room it was my job to maintain a distance, a show. I was going to write. I'd write a letter. How good it is to sit in the window and drink. Light a cigarette, let your thoughts wander, they go up and down the streets and search for something in the city, in and out of doors, up and down stairs, like shadows; they live your life, mimic your voice and use your name. Slowly they assume the shape of a familiar form, they dress themselves in your clothes and raise their hands the way you raise your hand, they have taken over the things that are your habits. You sit at the window of your hotel room smoking a cigarette, he walks the city searching for something you don't want to acknowledge, as if he's taken over your secrets, your innermost impulses and darkest desires, as if he has turned them into a kind of motor, a mechanism, a driving force, an inner spring that winds him up and propels him down that street you ought not to go down. There he stands outside a door. He waits, lights a cigarette, so controlled and self-assured, without any doubts, he doesn't doubt, why should he? He wants to go through the door, up the stairs, he wants to go in to her. He waits his turn, looks at the time, his wristwatch, counts seconds and minutes without any concept of time, he counts, that's all. One, two, three, four, five, repeated over and over again. She descends on the count of three, with a man; he has a face similar to the face that's waiting, the shadow and the man, they shake hands, briefly greet one another. Are they acquainted? No, they don't know each other, how could they? Automatically they shake hands, replace each other, and he mounts the stairs the other came down. She undresses in the same way he just dressed. Off and on, on and off, like pushing a button, like your finger pressing a switch of skin, a birthmark? a nipple? a growth you squeeze and press, she opens her mouth. She says: let's cheat death. He repeats what she's said, presses his finger as hard as he can on the wart of her navel; is it a wound? a cut? an incision? the skin is bright red and wrinkled, she's been sewn together like a rag doll. Let's cheat death, he says and bends forward; you can see the shadow moving behind the curtains in the room, a hotel room, it looks like other rooms, a window, a bed, a mirror; and that's what you like most of all: that everything resembles something else. There is no loss, there is no death, no love or sorrow, just repetition and life. How good it is to sit at a window and smoke. I remember so well the first time I came to Paris, it seems like yesterday, I was seventeen. I came with my first girlfriend, she was sixteen, we'd been together for just over a year. I can't understand us being allowed to travel, how our parents let us go, sixteen and seventeen years old we went across Europe by train, first on a train from Bergen to Oslo, then on a night train via Copenhagen straight on to Hamburg where we changed into an express train that raced through Germany, day and night across great flat Germany and little flat Belgium, until we crossed the French border and arrived at the Gare du Nord in the evening. It was dark. We knew nothing about Paris, except what we'd read in magazines and books, that was enough; we wanted to go to Paris. We were in Paris, took the metro to the Latin Quarter, got out at St Michel, walked a hundred yards and found a hotel called St Severin, it had one star, a double room cost forty-eight francs. It was perfect. Apart from the fact that the hotel had no vacancies. The receptionist cast a blatantly appraising eye over us, weren't we old enough? We were hungry and weary enough, we were dirty and confused enough, we were desperate and had money enough; we had to have a hotel room. We have a room that isn't like the other rooms, said the receptionist. We don't usually let it out, it's a room reserved for regular customers, during the day, you can use it tonight and change rooms early tomorrow morning. I'm doing you a favour, welcome to Paris, he gave us the key and a polite bow, as if we were now about to make a big mistake. The room was at the top of the building, we took the lift up, fifth floor. We clasped each other. I'll go down and buy a bottle of wine and a few baguettes, then we'll celebrate in our room, celebrate that we've arrived, we're in Paris, I said. I know that, she said. We humped our packs and unlocked the door of the room.

It was large and red. Red lighting, red wallpaper with red flowers; climbing roses. A dark brown carpet on the floor, a double bed with a wine-red bedspread. Above the bed, on the ceiling was a large mirror, it spanned the entire the bed. On the left side of the bed, on the wall, another rectangular mirror; lying in bed would be like being in a red box where we could see ourselves from several directions and angles. We stood in the doorway, as if neither of us wanted to cross the threshold that separated us from the room; this is no good, she said, we can't sleep here. I embraced her for a second time; we must, I said. We've only got to turn off the light, and then it'll be completely dark. She shook her head, I could see she was trembling; do you know what sort of room this is? she asked. Yes, I know, I said. We can open the window, sit on the windowsill, the room's bound to have a fantastic view, it's only for one night, I said. Now I'm going down to buy wine and something to eat, we are in Paris, I said. I know that, she said. Don't open the door to anyone except me, I joked; I'll knock three times. I ran down the stairs and out into the streets; there was an explosion of faces and lighted windows, voices and bodies, all walking, I walked through a stream, it was night in Paris and everything was open, restaurants and bars, shops and kiosks. I bought something to eat and drink, and stuffed it into a paper bag wanting to hurry back to the hotel room, elated and in love, it was as if something had blossomed anew; she wasn't the same, I wasn't the same, we were in a strange city, a great city, a nocturnal city, we were in Paris. I knocked twice on the door. Who is it? she asked. It's me, I'm here at the appointed hour, I said, assuming a deeper, disguised voice. She opened the door cautiously, red light, she'd changed and pinned up her hair. I can't let you in, she said, I'm waiting for someone else, he was to knock three times, I'm busy, I've got an appointment. It's me, I said. Are you the one called Jean? she asked. It's me, I said. You knocked twice, she said, and I didn't recognize your voice, but come in, it doesn't really matter who you are and what you're called anyway. My name is Jean, like everyone else, as agreed, I said and entered the room, she'd pulled the counterpane off the bed; white pillows, white sheets. Has there been anyone here before me? I asked. It's a quiet evening, and you're lucky, she said. I can see that, I said. How old are you? I'm sixteen, she said. Sixteen, that's barely adult, are you new here? I'm completely new, she said. This wouldn't be your first time, would it? I asked. No, it isn't my first time, think this is your lucky day or something? You talk as if you've got experience, I said, sixteen and old already, a year for every man, that's quite an age, eh? I don't think like that, I think of age in terms of love, we're only as old as the person we love, she said. And if the person you love is older than you, if he's had a lot of women? She cast her gaze down, I could see her face reddening, a blush, she blushed so easily, it was one of the things I loved about her, that blush. I'm in love with only one person, she said, and he's just like me, the same age, it's only me he loves. You can never be sure of that, I said, he could have others without your knowledge, you can never be quite certain. If you think he wants anyone except me, she said, suddenly angry, then I'll stop seeing him right now. Right this moment? Right this moment! she said. He could be with someone else as we speak, I said. And thinking that the girl he's with is more beautiful than the first, raunchier and feistier, more flaunting and not so hesitant, not so innocent. She reddened again, but this time partly from anger, there was a fine mottling of scarlet on her throat and face, a rash, I'd never seen it before. Are you saying he prefers this tart to his girlfriend? she asked. You never know, I said. She sat down on the bed, I could see she had tears in her eyes, it was a dangerous game we were playing, I'd thought of stopping, but just then she held out her hand; I want to be paid, she said. I want to see how much you're willing to pay for a sixteen-year-old slut who talks dirty and opens her legs when you ask her to. I won't pay anything at all, I said, let's stop this stupid game, it's all because of this dreadful room, I don't like it, I said. But I like it, she said. I want to see your money, give it to me, you'll have to open your wallet. I went towards her, tried to embrace her, but she pushed me away. Don't touch me, she hissed, not until you've paid. First I want to see what I'm paying for, I said. I want to see you naked, and then you must tell me what you can do, then I'll pay you what you're worth. She hesitated, looked steadily at me as I stood over her, whether there was disdain or desire in that look, it was impossible to say, but the look was different, I no longer recognized it. She got up from the bed, walked resolutely to the window and pulled off her skirt. She had nothing on underneath, unbuttoned her blouse and dropped it on the floor. Then she got up on the table and sat facing me with legs apart. I can do a bit of everything, she said and raised her hips from the table top. Up and down, slowly, I didn't know where she'd picked the movements up, if she'd seen them, or if she'd got them from herself, from another place inside herself, an alien place, a secret place, a much older place, a far more dangerous place, she put her hand over her sex, spread her fingers then pushed the middle one between her labia. She was masturbating. Opened her mouth and showed me her tongue; here I am, she said, a real slut, your slut, I want to see your money, count it out, she said. I pulled out all the money I had from my pocket, a hundred, two hundred, three hundred, three hundred and sixty-five francs; it's not enough, she shouted. It's all I've got, I said. In your bag, she said, the Norwegian money, count it and hold it out, let me see how much, let me see how much I'm worth, she said. I went towards her, wanting to stop her, hold her, but she screamed; I'll scream even louder if you touch me, if you come closer before I've seen the money. I got out the bag and the money, it was my emergency money, in thousand kroner notes, I held out the first. It's not enough, she said. She'd got up on the table, with her back to me, bending forward, still with her fingers between her legs, it was turning me mad, insane, I wasn't myself any more, she was no longer herself, we were two different people and it was too late to turn back, we had crossed a line and I didn't know if it was possible to return; we're losing each other, I thought, but I couldn't stop holding out the money, I put it on the table beneath her, two thousand, three thousand, three thousand three hundred and sixty-five, I said, please, I said; I begged and implored her; that's more like it, she said. Three thousand, that's fine, that's enough, that's OK, she said and I heard her come. She shuddered and her muscles quivered, she sank down on to her hands and knees and turned her head back towards me; now you can have me, she said.

The Rimbaud route

A hotel room. Light, innocent, clean, and yet filled with so many meetings, so many stories and dreams, you dream. You sleep. You wake, sit up in bed; where? When? Who? Morning. Alone. Sunlight, window, a door. Shadows, a tree, the street below, a crossroads. A good room. A light clean room, you hear sounds in the room next door. You imagine a man and a woman. I opened the door, and out of the neighbouring room emerged a stout elderly man in a suit, followed by a youth wearing overalls and a workman's shirt. They were lovers. I heard them, the heavy breath above the light, the small voice under the big, like a piece of music; the cries of love, of ecstasy, ah, so good, so good, more, more, I like it. The young man and the elderly one, they greeted me politely when I put my head out into the corridor, as if they'd dressed themselves in a new identity, their everyday clothes, the business man and the artisan, they followed each other down the stairs and out into the street, stopped, shook hands and went their separate ways. Where was I going? I was leaving the city, leaving Paris, back to the car at Charleville-Mézières. I packed my writing materials into my shoulder bag, had coffee down in the small breakfast room behind reception, paid for the room and set out along the route I will call the Rimbaud Route, from the title of an anthology by Marc Cholodenko: *La tentation du trajet Rimbaud.* Arthur Rimbaud was born in Charleville-Mézières and grew up there together with his mother and three siblings, until at the age of fifteen he ran away for the first time. His first escape, one of many he would subsequently make to Paris. As a rule he walked there and back, on feet like the wind, with his hat and pipe, a short, threadbare coat, long hair, long legs, already a Bohemian and wild man, a rebel, a poet and visionary: 'I say this to you: the poet must be a prophet, must turn himself into a prophet. He turns himself into a prophet through a long, systematic confusion of all his senses. All forms of love, suffering and madness; he ransacks himself, he ingests all poisons until only meaning remains,' wrote Rimbaud in one of the extraordinary letters he sent proving that as a fifteen year old he was a mature poet: 'Now I wallow in as much filth as possible. Why? I want to be a poet, and I'm working at making myself a visionary. You wouldn't be able to understand this, and I don't know how to explain it to you. It involves arriving at the unknown through a confusion of all the senses. The suffering is enormous, one must be strong, be a born poet, and I have discovered that I am a poet. It isn't my fault. It's wrong to say: I conceive. One ought to say: I am conceived.

'I am someone else.

'So much the worse for the forest if it discovers that it's a violin, and devil take the blockheads who argue about things they don't understand.'

And even earlier, on 2 November 1870, to his teacher and friend Georges Izambard: 'I'm dying, rotting away amongst vulgarity, pettiness and drab melancholy. What shall I do, I who am quite determined to cultivate that great freedom . . . I thought of setting out once more; I could have done it: I had new clothes, I could have sold my watch, and long live freedom! But I didn't go! I didn't go! I often find I want to set off. Come hat, coat, my two hands in their pockets, and so off! Away!'

Few have done as much walking as Arthur Rimbaud, he was the poet who wore out his legs, at the age of thirty-seven he got problems with his right knee and had to have his right leg amputated. By that time he'd been on the road since he was fifteen, he'd gone his ways in France, Belgium, England, Italy and Africa; it's said that he lead his many caravans on foot, while the others rode, Rimbaud wanted to spare the mule and the camel, he walked and made walking a way of life; he wasn't just a seer, a poet, an adventurer and explorer, arms dealer and photographer, cartographer and rejuvenator of the French language, he was also a walker, a wanderer:

Seen enough. Same sights beneath all skies.
Had enough. Noises from the towns at night, and
always in the sun.

Known enough. Life's stopping places. Oh, sounds and sights!

Departures in new abandonment and new tumult.

The poem 'Striking Camp' was part of the collection *Illuminations*, the last Rimbaud completed, before he bid farewell to poetry at the age of twenty. At nineteen he'd completed *A Season in Hell*, the book that would make him one of the most important poets of French literature, he wrote most of the anthology at Roche, his mother's birthplace, a small village north of Vouziers and south of Charleville. I arrived at Roche after four days' walk, northwards from Paris, through the Champagne district and via Reims, entered the village late in the afternoon, asked for the Rimbaud house and found it at a crossroads; a two-storey brick house with green shutters, closed. In this house Rimbaud had paced the first floor, stamping and banging out the rhythms of the poems he was writing while he roared and wept. It frightened his mother and kept her awake at night, but when the writing was finished she paid for the book's printing, and when she read it and didn't understand any of it and asked her son how the book should be read, he answered that it was to be read literally. 'The weak and the old are so respectable they're begging to be boiled.' Was this aimed at his mother? Did she take it literally? It wasn't difficult, outside the building in Roche, to imagine the scenes that took place between mother and son in that small house; I stood in the garden in front of the door with its plate that announced that it was here that Arthur Rimbaud wrote *A Season in Hell*, and only then did it strike me as I stood in front of the house, that I'd found the place that was the starting point for my own writing: the house where the young boy lived with his mother. The young boy who wanted to rebel, to leave, go off, live that great freedom. The young boy who wanted to write. Who wanted to live a wild and poetic life. Who wanted to see, who wanted to walk. The Rimbaud Route.

I had trodden it in my own way, a journey not all that fast, not all that difficult and uncompromising, but I had taken that route; I stood here in front of the house in Roche, and could call myself an author. Darkness was falling. I had to start searching for a place to sleep. I continued along my route, walking in the dark, was I scared? No, I wasn't scared, I'd become used to the dark and to sleeping out, but nonetheless it was different walking in darkness than in daylight, not just because the light had gone, but because everything was more distinct; the tall trees and the leaves that rustled in the wind, a large boulder with cracks and holes, a clearing in the wood, the sounds and the country, I saw and heard everything more clearly when it was dark. The opening, the spring, I heard it before I saw it. In front of me, opening up, the distance between the sounds became greater, quieter, no, calmer, it became calmer. In front of me, a silence, an opening, I could hear it, sense it, as if I were approaching a special place. I was approaching a special place. Now I could see it; a clearing, and there was the chapel behind a pool of still water. A spring. The water lay still in a stone cistern, shaped like a cross. Or like two arms, you bent down and drank the water. The water wasn't still after all, it sprang from the earth and ran away through a thin subterranean artery. The movements of the water; I couldn't see them, but I heard the water running, underground, a faint laughter.

I had never before, in any place, experienced such tranquillity.

This was where I wanted to sleep. I found a suitable tree, spread my jacket as a groundsheet and lay down with my head towards the trunk. From where I lay I could see the chapel and the pool; I was weary and wanted to sleep, but I couldn't sleep. The silence, the perfect peace, kept me awake. The peace, the perfect silence, disturbed me, woke me, I was wide awake. I realized I wouldn't get to sleep. I sat up, lit a cigarette, and then I saw the bats, they gathered in formation above the tree and dived, hurtling down towards the place where I was sitting. Inquisitive? They repeated the action, in a circle, re-established the forma- tion and dived, dashing down to where I sat. Again and again, a little closer each time, nearer and nearer it seemed. Did they want to inspect me, find out what I was, who I was? Had they formed an image, suddenly they flew away. I was alone, but was I? I waited, but for what? I'd been inspected, what was it that was going to appear? I'd been notified, who was it, what was it that was going to reveal itself? I kept my eye on the spring, tried to see into the wood, a hare? a fox? A movement, no, nothing. Silence. Peace. I don't believe I've ever been so wide awake before. I had a bottle of spirits in my bag, for sleepless nights, I needed it now. I drank from the bottle, smoked cigarettes, nothing happened. So why couldn't I sleep? Why was I kept awake? The hours passed (did time have anything to do with it?), the night passed, it wore away; I sat under the tree and watched it go while I waited for something else to happen. Nothing happened.

Was it this nothing that kept me awake?

Was it this nothing that was the point of this vigil, in a place where anything could happen?

How do you relate to nothing?

You wait. You think. You smoke, drink, do ordinary things as if everything were normal. You are about to vanish, disappear for ever perhaps, and still you behave as if you'll go on living, as if you can't die. You smoke and drink, you sit and wait, you don't know what you're waiting for.

I smoked and drank, talked aloud to myself. I said: this is without doubt the most beautiful place you've ever been in. So peaceful, so quiet, so filled with nothing. Could this be the place you've dreamt of, time and time again, ever since you were a child and a teenager; a place you've never been to and never seen, but which has popped up in your dreams as a place you know, a familiar place, a place that was waiting, that one day would come? Is this it? Is this the place? Have you finally found the place, as when a dream comes true? Could this be the place of death?

I leapt up. I sprang to my feet. What if I'd gone to sleep? I jumped up and down, heart thudding, pulse racing, but my blood seemed frozen to ice, I was cold. My right foot had gone to sleep, half dead, on its way to death, I flapped my arms and beat life into my limbs. On with my jacket, bag over my shoulder, quickly away, I jogged out of the wood, without turning, walked as fast as I could in the direction of the path and found the road; I walked as if I were pursued. Like someone who's just escaped. Away, striding out, along the road; it swung and rippled on through the morning-still landscape with its fields and prominences. A hilltop, trees and a church, buildings and streets, a village, Omont, sleeping. Another wood, a narrow path, through birch and aspen, birds and leaves, that riotous unseen chirping and singing, nature's insanity, just before dawn.

The sun rose. Again I found the river, the Meuse, rejoined the route I had travelled in the opposite direction going to Paris, now I was headed for Charleville, a day's journey, about twenty miles, and I'd be there. Once there, I'd have a good bath. I'd eat a good meal. I'd drink a good bottle of wine; visit a good bar and sleep in a good bed. I wanted to rest. Write. Sit at the window of the bed and breakfast with its view over the fantastic Place Ducale. The sun hung low at the end of the road, I walked towards the sun, it glittered in the river, the trout leapt, jumping for insects and making rings in the water, the calm River Meuse; it was like coming across an old acquaintance, a friend, the Meuse, good morning Meuse, how are you, Meuse? The river would take me to Nouvion-sur-Meuse, where I could get breakfast; a cup of coffee, white bread and marmalade, maybe a soft-boiled egg, I walked and fantasized; today's newspapers, a glass of orange juice. A piece of cheese. A pear. A glass of dry white wine. A small pie, a piece of cake, a glass of apple brandy. I passed a man with a fishing rod, he was standing on the riverbank, staring down into the water. A half-full bucket of water for storing the fish, a little metal box with earth and live worms; he threaded the worm on to the sharp hook, swung his rod and cast. Good morning. He followed the river with his eyes, waiting. His hat was pulled down over his eyes, the shade enabled him to follow the movements in the river. In his hatband he'd stuck hooks and flies. A fishing bag across his shoulder, a knife in his belt, this was his equipment, the tools he required for fishing. A Thermos of coffee, a lunch-box. Tobacco. What did he remind me of? It struck me that the patience of the fisherman resembled my own; it's the patience of the writer, I thought. You sit at a desk and wait. So there isn't much difference between him and me, I thought and greeted him in return. Good morning. The same patience. The same concentration. The same expectations. I wanted to slap him amicably on the shoulder, but I didn't. I missed my writing.

It was a good sign. I was on the right road. I was on the road home. The man with the fishing rod had reminded me about my work. The pleasure of sitting at my writing table. The pencils, pens, the typewriter. A thermo-jug of coffee, sandwiches, cigarettes. I wanted to go home. I walked more calmly now, more slowly, I had shaken off that shadow of nothingness. The sun was high in the sky, the air was clear and pure, no clouds, the heat arrived with the sun, I sweated. Undid my jacket and shirt. Sunflowers and poppies. The path became broader, a towpath, horses had towed boats upstream along it; the river had locks, a small house stood by each set of gates, like a station building along a railway line, they'd been turned into modern homes. A garden, a fence, a dog that hurled itself at the netting. A Rottweiler. Lilies and chrysanthemums. Behind the fence, on a terrace near the house, a family sat having breakfast. The apple trees were in blossom, white petals, which fell from the boughs and formed white circles round the trunks. You needn't be frightened of the dog, it's not dangerous. The woman might have been the mother, she called: where are you going? I'm on my way home, I said. But where's home, you're not from round here, said the mother. I'm from Norway, I said. Are you walking all the way to Norway? she who must have been the mother asked, but I made no reply, I'd already left the house behind.

How does a journey begin?

How does a journey begin? I'm lying on the sofa reading, two comfortable cushions behind my head, a woollen rug over my legs, a cold day in March, it's raining and the rain turns to hail; it drums on the windowpanes. Chinks of sunlight. At half past eleven the post arrives, I can see the postman's car from my window; I only have to raise my head, there's the post. This journey begins on the sofa. I've decided to stay put, stay put for an entire spring so that I can write and do what I like doing most of all: sitting by the window looking out. Seeing how the frost leaves the earth, how the snow covers the grass in the garden and is gone again after only a few hours' mild weather. Snowdrops and daffodils push up out of the ground and open; it seems like a miracle each time it happens, each spring, in March. Every year on the fourteenth of the month the wagtail arrives; I sit and wait for it. But now the post comes, it's half past eleven, I raise my head almost automatically, and there's the postman's car on its way, it halts as usual by the stand of mailboxes, and I wait until the postman has distributed the post in the boxes, then I get up, lay aside the book I'm reading, leave the sofa and go out. The journey begins here; I leave the sofa and go out. A chilly feel to the air, a slight wind in the trees, I walk down the gravel path to the small tarmac road that passes the house, halt at the mailboxes, this is one of the highlights of the day: opening the box and taking out the post. A letter. It stands out; a battered envelope, as if it has been through many hands, as if it has come a long way; it's from abroad. Austria. A wavy postmark and a portrait of Mozart on the stamp, it makes me happy. The letter is from Narve Skaar, my travelling companion. He's in Vienna. I make a cup of tea, add a little milk, slot the cassette of Mozart's clarinet concerto into the player: I'm ready to read the letter.

Half an hour later I'm ready to travel. I need to book flights, deal with a few practical matters, and make certain arrangements with my family such as it is; I'll be away several months. I'm to meet Narve Skaar in Athens. During the next few days, over the Internet, we find a place to meet and agree on a date by email: Neon Cafeteria, 18 March at 6 p.m. My plane lands in Athens at 16.35. I've underestimated the route from the airport to the city centre; the traffic is horrendous and there's virtual gridlock. By quarter to six I've had enough, push my way up to the bus driver, pat his shoulder and ask him to open the doors. I jump out. Walk as fast as I can towards the centre of Athens. It doesn't take me long to find the underground; I ask directions, get on the train indicated, get off at the recommended station, run up the stairs and emerge into an open square: the first thing I see is the sign announcing that

I've found the Neon Cafeteria. It's there on the other side of the square, directly opposite; I feel a wild exultation inside me. I stand for a few minutes overcome by the sight, the open square, the people, the traffic, the old buildings ranged in a semi-circle in the sun: it's the first time I've been to Athens.

It's quarter past six, I'm fifteen minutes late; this means that Narve Skaar will have drunk his first beer alone. I cross the square, go through the door; a crowd of people in a large locale with thick wooden tables and old chandeliers hanging from the ceiling, a beer hall almost, but with dinner service and waiters dressed in black, a stout, elderly woman sits on a sort of throne in the middle of the establishment; she's the cashier. At one of the tables I see the letter writer, he's reading. Making notes. A glass of beer on the table in front of him, a packet of cigarettes, his blue windproof over a white shirt, I notice that he's sunburnt. He's looking good. Denim trousers and brown leather boots, he's been travelling for more than three months, trudging round northern Europe on foot, high and low, cities and mountains, until it was time to make a decision; should he go home? Or head south? That was when he penned his letter, in a hotel room in Vienna: would I meet him in Athens? Would I join him in a walking trip from Delphi north towards the mountains and monasteries of Metéora, and later southwards from Antalya on what's known as the 'Lycian Way', an established long-distance route around the south coast of Turkey? His letter made me anxious, irritable and nervous; those are the symptoms, you're getting ready to travel.

I put on my usual suit, the walking suit, a blue wool suit with silver stripes; the gypsy suit, a black shirt, light mountain boots, Italian, yellow suede, waterproof boots of the very best quality, an orange mountain sack, sixty litres, lightly packed. And here I was, hungry and thirsty, in a watering hole in Athens. Narve Skaar was sitting at one of the tables waiting; we'd got a lot to talk about. For us there's nothing better than sitting at a table talking and drinking, smoking cigarettes and arguing. Athens is one of Narve's favourite cities, I can't understand why, my first impression is that the city seems chaotic and ruined by traffic and lack of planning. But Narve wants to show me the city, or in other words, his version of the city; all cities can be made sense of in different ways, you find your own spots; a small park with an outdoor restaurant, a street of booksellers, a corner where nuts and liquor are sold. A terrace on the hill below the Acropolis where you get a panorama of the city. A two-storey building, a narrow circular staircase from which we're shown out on to a balcony. It's just big enough for a table and two chairs, we order meatballs and retsina, cheese and a half bottle of ouzo. Athens lies beneath us like an inverted starry sky; lights from the houses and streets and from the cars that fly out of their trajectories like excitable shooting stars. I feel like making a wish. There is a jukebox in the restaurant, we go in and feed it coins, old singles; 'Make me smile' by Cockney Rebel. 'Too much in the skies', Annette Peacock. 'The things we do for love', 10CC. I want 'Rest in peace' by Mott the Hoople, the music and the voices, the cigarette smoke and the faces, young, as if time has stood still, as if we're still two young boys out for the first time and are bowled over by everything we see and hear. Travel doesn't make us older, it makes us younger. Travel confuses us, puts time and the years out of kilter, we imagine we're seeing everything with new eyes, with young eyes, and travel disrupts the memory, it makes us forget; we no longer recall our real age and the mistakes we've made and all the disappointments we've faced, we travel and believe we travel back to the time of our youth, while in fact we're sitting there dreaming. We dream, and travel demands this of us, it demands that we be young. Travel demands that we take in the world with an unclouded gaze, a young gaze, that we will view novelties with inquisitive and eager eyes, and we're more than willing to be persuaded and seduced, we're travelling back in time, back to our youth. We believe we have a right to eternal youth, and journeys ask for nothing in return except that we forget and dream. It's not difficult. We only have to choose a city, find a place with music and a view, drink enough wine and ouzo, join a discussion with strangers, young faces, scantily clad girls, boys with long hair and paperbacks in their pockets, talk about politics and literature, Antonio Gramsci and Pier Paolo Pasolini, and we're back in a lost time. A rediscovered time; we've come in from the balcony and joined what has developed into a party in the middle of the restaurant, a discussion around the table; is the revolution still possible? How to rebel and who will organize the new society? A revolution involving the entire world, it would begin in Greece, cradle of democracy, hotbed of change, home of revolution, but would it be able to crush the capitalism of the US and sweep away injustice in China? And what about Muslim countries, are they ready for a revolution in favour of Greek ideals? Formulated in Athens, one Thursday night in March, by wine-flown youngsters? No, we say. Haven't we read *Symposium*? Isn't that a revolutionary book, hasn't that changed the world? No, we say. Don't we realize that Plato was wrong in *Republic*, and right in *Symposium*? —All change springs from Eros, and love is revolution's true aim. Haven't we read Shakespeare's *A Midsummer Night's Dream*? The action takes place in Athens and is a great celebration of the potential of love. Shakespeare acknowledges the triumph of love, a new beginning for mankind. And the beginning begins, as always, in Athens. All right then, we say. We've let ourselves be persuaded and convinced, by Socrates and Shakespeare, by the youth of Athens, and suddenly we find ourselves in the midst of revolution, the heart of change, yes, now at last we're in Athens. The city of youth. The city of dreamers.

It's nearly three o'clock, the lights are switched on and off. The revolution has only just begun, but the restaurant is closing, and sadly we must take leave of our new friends.

Well, where do we sleep? I ask.

We've got a couple of beds in a hostel, in a dormitory for eight, we'll sleep like two soldiers, Narve says.

That sounds good. That sounds as if the journey has begun, I say.

Early tomorrow, at ten-thirty, the bus leaves for Delphi, and that's where our walk starts, we'll be following a route across the mountains that's two and a half thousand years old. I'll show you the map in the morning.

The map is plain and imprecise. But Greek maps are better than Turkish ones, the latter turn out to be unusable, as maps are in countries where the army decides where you can and can't go, what you can and can't see. Judging by its maps Greece is freer and more accessible than Turkey, but less accommodating and open than countries in which we're used to roaming relatively freely using maps that supply the truth rather than fine approximations.

But the best maps cannot be bought, they're drawn by people you meet along the way. And people you meet along the way are both accommodating and precise. This is true of all countries. The best maps are conveyed orally and by gestures, occasionally with a pen and a scrap of paper. Sometimes the informal guide will come along too to show just where the road makes that imperceptible fork, that difficult turn, and in this way you become acquainted with the landscape and the roads using a method that is both direct and accurate; a short cut, a secret path, we all know these routes that nobody else knows. They're our routes, our own paths criss-crossing the drift of map and highway.

We're sitting on the terrace outside the hotel room we've found at Delphi studying the maps (accredited by the Greek Army Geographical Service), and from where we're sitting on the high ground we can see right down to the port of Itéa and the point where the Corinthian Gulf enters the strait dividing the mainland from the Peloponnese, and meets the Gulf of Patraikós in the Ionian Sea. To the left, behind us, the village of Delphi climbs the mountainside that rises steeply from the Temple of Apollo and the spring where the Oracle lived, to form a prominence above the village that continues to rise to four and a half thousand feet before the plateau flattens out and turns into a valley running all the way to Eptalofos, which is the first leg of our walking trip. We're drinking white wine and eating feta cheese and olives, a good night's sleep, an early start, and we'll be off on the temple road which will take us out of Delphi and up into the mountains.

A cold night, starry skies, we sleep with the balcony door open to get used to the temperature outside. A trial of sleeping bags and woollen underwear, of the blankets and clothes we're taking for walking at altitude. We haven't taken tents or insulating mats, neither of us likes the heavy, loaded packs so beloved of backpackers, we're both too vain to want to take anything we don't like with us; we'll manage in the old way, the simple way, we'll be cold. The night is freezing and we are cold, in the morning we agree to buy woolly hats and leather gloves, a bottle of whisky against the worst of the cold, the toughest, sleepless nights. But breakfast is hardly over before it starts to get hot. We leave the hotel room, strip off as we walk through the village, off with our jackets, off with our sweaters and woollen socks, we're sweating. The main problem isn't the cold or the heat, but the huge variations in temperature. The temperature climbs as we do, an ascent of two and a half thousand feet in more than twenty degrees of heat, and it will get hotter, it's going to be hot.

But the sun is still low and gentle, we walk up from the village and find the path that takes us past gardens and through olive groves, past stone buildings with red tiled roofs, up to the first hill where we get a marvellous view across Delphi and the valley opening out to the sea, towards Itéa and the Corinthian Gulf. Up here we join the ancient temple road, a marked transition; the path turns into a paved way a yard wide where the outer stones, a kerb against the valley below, are bigger than the sporadic slabs, between grass and gravel, in the middle of the way. A magnificent road, two and a half thousand years old, it makes regular, long sweeps up the mountainside before describing a turn, a masterpiece of stonemasonry and curve formation, a master bend, a miracle of a turn to the left, followed by another straight of about a hundred yards, and then a hairpin to the right; in this way the road zigzags up, it coils upwards, like a colossal snake. Ah, the snake, the tale about the snake, which we hear as we go, told us by a historian, we catch up with him and his wife, a couple, taking their regular morning walk. Ah, trekking in a suit, he comments as I'm about to pass them. Are you going far? We tell them how far we're going and where we're from. Ah! He once gave a lecture at the University of Oslo, on Aesop's fables, he points, at that very spot down there, he says, Aesop was stoned to death by the inhabitants of Delphi, they recognized themselves in his fables and felt ridiculed. Do you know the fable of the snake? The snake's stomach was tired of being led the whole time by the snake's head, it began to complain, it wanted to decide for a change, the stomach wanted to decide where the snake would slither, what the snake would do. The head was fed up with all the stomach's moaning and decided to let the stomach decide for a bit, but during this period everything went wrong, the stomach was only interested in food and all the other things it craved, and this led the snake astray, it got lost and finally ended up in a place where there was neither food nor anything to drink. The snake was starving, it was close to death. Now you see what happens when you make the decisions, said the head to the stomach.

We laugh heartily at this fable. I decide to buy *Aesop's Fables* during the journey and I did find an English edition in a bookshop in Eptalofos. But I couldn't find that fable. It didn't exist in the English edition, nor in any of the editions I looked at subsequently, in fact it wasn't one of the fables Aesop had written, and I wondered if the historian hadn't perhaps invented the fable, regarding himself as a latter-day Aesop, and that it was an improvisation about us, the two wanderers in ridiculous costumes, mindlessly heading for the great adventure?

We're standing right above where Aesop is supposed to have been stoned, and the new Aesop relates one of his fables which makes us laugh long and loud. We laugh as we walk, Narve says: I can be the head and you can be the stomach, and we must co-operate. What says the stomach? I say: well, we'll have to stop soon for a break and something to eat. What says the head? The head says that we haven't walked far enough. We can have a drink of water, but we must wait with the food until we've got half way. Has the head remembered to stow the wine bottles in his pack? Yes, the head has brought along two bottles of white wine, and we can drink one with the food. The head travels six feet four inches above the ground, he swings along the road, on long legs, a comely gait, I think. The sun beats down. We get out our sunglasses and light caps, walk through snow-capped mountains and follow crystal-clear streams, a river, the old temple road has become a more modern gravel track which gradually turns into a path; we cross bogs and grass, an open valley which leads us into a narrow forest road. On the edge of the trees is a farm, and outside the main building is a horse. As soon as it glimpses us it gallops up, halts and bites me on the shoulder. Impulsively, I strike out at its neck with all my strength, it backs. I attempt to frighten it off, but it stands there. I examine my shoulder, but its teeth haven't pierced my skin. We carry on walking, the horse following. The farm is deserted, no car, shutters over the windows. The horse follows us for several miles, we agree to try to shake it off; on a narrow piece of rising ground Narve turns and goes back along the path, which one of us will the horse follow? It follows Narve, our plan has succeeded, he walks slowly back and at a certain point he'll turn again, leave the path and sprint back up to me, walking ahead. Half an hour later Narve comes running, he rejoins me, we march quickly away and after a few minutes the horse catches up with us. It follows us for a long time, we've walked for four hours and are over half way; the place where we should eat. What should we do? We're hungry and tired of this blasted horse. Is it going to follow us all the way to Eptalofos, into the village, are we supposed to take it to the restaurant? The head suggests that we should give it some whisky, that we should set it drunk, but the stomach says no. He's afraid of brawls and unpleasantness. He's never fought a drunken horse before, nor even a sober one, but he'd prefer the latter. He kicks the horse, gets it in the ribs, it rears up on its hind legs and whinnies. This makes the head cross, not with the horse, but with the stomach. Leave it alone, he says. We walk in silence. The horse follows. We walk through snow, we've reached four and a half thousand feet and soon we'll begin the descent towards Eptalofos; it's heavy going. The sun has gone down, it's getting dark and the air is starting to turn cold, we're sweating. We've been walking for six hours, our reserves and energy are depleted. We reach the main road in the dusk, a gravel road from the mountain village to a ski centre high up; there's a large car on the side of the road, a Range Rover, it's stuck in the snow. As soon as we see the car we both have the same idea. We walk towards the car, offer to help the driver out of the snowdrift asking at the same time if he can give the horse something to eat as it's hungry. The children in the back seat feed the horse chocolate and other sweets, we push the car out of the snow, say goodbye and sneak off. The horse remains by the car. We make a rapid getaway, trot down a short cut through the forest, find a clearing and lie down in the lee of a rock, we've got to eat. Hungry and thirsty, we attack the food and drink like savages. We can see the road from where we're sitting, and sure enough, we witness something we'll never forget, a fantastic sight; we laugh so much we stop eating: the Range Rover going at full speed down the narrow, twisting gravel road, with the horse galloping after it.

Eptalofos at last. An idyllic little mountain village of wooden houses and pitched roofs, narrow streets and lights in windows. Snow is falling and we must find a place to sleep. It's the weekend, all the hotels are full, the receptionist at Hotel Tsarouchas says there isn't a bed anywhere, he has phoned round for us; everywhere is full, he says in German. We're not German, I tell him. We can sleep behind the reception desk, we can sleep in the cleaning cupboard, we can sleep anywhere, I tell him. At that young Tsarouchas phones his mother, she has a spare room, it was his bedroom as a boy, we can sleep there, if that's good enough for us. It's more than good enough for us. We thank him. We thank him again and order a large meal in the hotel restaurant; we consume meatballs and fried potatoes and two bottles of red wine. After the meal we sit in front of the fire with young Tsarouchas describing our walk across the mountains. It was tougher than we'd imagined, four seasons in one hike, when we started it was spring and now it's winter already; we're sitting in front of the fire in the grate and are looking out through the big window at the snow settling on all that darkness. Stratos Tsarouchas has black, slicked hair and an angular face with a large nose and wide mouth, he sips his whisky and listens, paying just enough attention to us, at the same time keeping an eye on reception and the guests in the dining room, beautiful young Greek women and men, sitting in groups; the sound of cutlery on porcelain, low-cut dresses, voices and laughter, it makes me tired and content, I nod off and fall asleep in my chair. A car is called and we're driven to Tsarouchas' mother and the house where we're to sleep.

Two beds. Brown wallpaper with a floral pattern on the opposite wall, wooden walls, a door out to the bathroom which is moss green. We're inhabiting an imitation of nature. We shower, lie naked on our beds and smoke, drink from the whisky bottle. Tomorrow we're walking to Lilaia. It's a little under half the distance we walked today, mostly downhill, an easy stage. Our clothes are hanging in the bathroom to dry, they smell of horse and effort, sweat and moss; we are no imitations of nature.

We are woken by Stratos. His mother has made breakfast, we eat in the kitchen with the Tsarouchas family: Elena and Kosta, their daughter Lia, who's younger than Stratos, nineteen perhaps, the same nose and mouth as her brother, but with lighter hair, dyed, presumably. Her mother's hair and her father's face, her own sullen supercilious expression. Youth. Prejudices. We still smell of the outdoors and the gypsy life, help ourselves enthusiastically to the simple breakfast; strong coffee, scrambled eggs, coarse bread and a yoghurt-like milk. A good meal. A lovely family; I photograph them, they pose by the kitchen table, their arms around each other.

In the village I purchase an English edition of *Aesop's Fables*, we buy food and get two litre bottles of water. Three elderly men are sitting in the square cooking soup in large pots which steam over an open fire, it's Saturday and the feast before Lent; the soup is made from vegetables and goat's meat. Small globules of olive oil and whole peppercorns, the taste of thyme, garlic and bay leaves, we eat the soup with a glass of homemade liquorice brandy, our foreheads are marked with ash and we make our way out of Eptalofos slightly tipsy. People who walk know that it's often harder and less satisfying to walk downhill than up, a descent is a strain on the knees and back, and walking downhill is almost always less interesting than climbing up, I don't know why, perhaps walking upwards is synonymous with a beginning, the beginning of something new. Coming down is sadder, more depressing, we're walking towards something resembling an end, presumably the descent conjures up thoughts of death, in the same way as the trip up engenders a feeling of potential and new life. We must learn to find the same delight in going down as going up, Narve says and tries to find things to take pleasure in; a wood seen from above, the tints of silver and grey in the slate roofs and the smoke from the chimneys that seems to bid us welcome. The view of the valley and village which we can already see below us. Maybe the downward journey is exhausting because we can see the things we'll pass long before we get to them; there's the bend we'll shortly round, here's the path through the wood which we saw from above, now comes the monastery as expected, and here we see the monastery garden which we've already carefully inspected from the hill. We walk down. Follow the main road, it doesn't take long before we feel the blisters, the burning under the soles of our feet and the backache. Our knees ache, our shoulders. Our heads ache. An attack of tedium, the sovereign remedy for this, says the doctor's son, an antidote to the depressing effect of descent, is a medicine that has the opposite effect. The only heartening analgesic that has an enlivening effect, Narve says, is alcohol. Fine. So we'll go down and drink up, this leads us into the game we often amuse ourselves with on strenuous routes; he's Doctor Drink and I'm Professor Puff. What's your opinion, doctor? I ask. We need another drink, he says. What say you, professor? I believe tobacco will be beneficial. In what way beneficial? Tobacco has an animating effect, says the professor. Where did you study, sir? asks the doctor. At the University of Bergen, sir, says the professor. This makes both the doctor and the professor laugh. And you? At the Faculty of History in the same university. But, surely, that can hardly have qualified you as a medical man, I say. My patients are mainly from the nineteenth century, he says. As indeed are your methods, sir, I rejoin. No matter, sir, they're still most efficacious, he says. Yes, the drink has its effect, our mood improves, we're soon down, walking the final stretch on the path which is a short cut through the woods. We emerge from the trees and meet the main round again at a bend, and around the bend there is an open space, and on the open space a celebration is in progress.

In the open space before Lilaia church, five long tables have been spread with white tablecloths. The families sitting at the tables have brought cutlery and glasses, food and drink from their own kitchens. A trumpet is being blown, a small Gypsy orchestra consisting of four men in dark suits and white shirts begins to play. A man dressed up as a clown is walking about on stilts, throwing marzipan balls down to the children. Little stalls are selling grilled meat and various kinds of cheese, sausages and the local soup; we advance towards one of the stalls, but are immediately beckoned over to a long table; there are vacant places at the end, chairs are found, we must taste the food of the Kalafatis family; there is a bean dish with cheese accompanied by marinated paprika, as well as small sausages and olives, homemade rosé wine and the usual ouzo, coffee and cakes with strawberries and raspberries in a sugary glaze which must be eaten with cream on top. The Kalafatis family consists of a father and mother, two sons and two daughters, their friends, grandparents and various uncles and aunts, toddlers and teenagers, they take up half the long table and sing Greek songs, occasionally getting drowned out by the Gypsy orchestra which plays faster and faster before being cut off by a storm of applause. We eat and drink, our packs are placed under the table, the family pet is constituted guard dog and lies lethargically at his post; we're going to dance. We dance with the Kalafatis girls. Gypsy music is characterised by starting fast and then accelerating at an ever increasing tempo, never moving on, but going round and round.

The music flies, it spins, it whirls, faster and faster, in a circle, as if it's in a hurry never to get anywhere; it bores down through the tarmac and makes a hole in the ground down which the dancers disappear, spiralling down, beneath the earth, down into the darkness and the netherworld to which the music finds its way and finds its home. A swift subterranean marriage. A brief union and a quick coalescing in the darkness where everything is beautiful and everything is good before the music whisks the wedded up through a whirling tunnel of light and laughter, hauling the dancers unwillingly up into the daylight where they are quickly separated and sent back, each to their own.

Back to the chairs and the table, to the food and wine, to the conversation and cigarettes. Back to the Kalafatis brothers. They offer us a lift to Gravia, a fifteen-minute drive, it would take about four hours to walk; we thank our hosts and hump our packs on to our backs, walk waving and unsteady back to the road where we belong.

Finding the way

We cross the spine of the Píndos Mountains, spending the nights in the Greek Tourist Association's huts, the first a log cabin with a woodstove and good beds, then an icy stone bothy with wooden ledges and woollen blankets which we wrap around our sleeping bags, and lie there tired and sleepless. Hard going, not enough sleep. The only food we have left in our packs is a bag of raisins and a bar of chocolate. We descend towards Kalambáka, a small town at the foot of the Metéora, that extraordinary chain of mountains with formations like gigantic sculptures or colossi hewn in a fit of divine madness. What is a mountain? Forces of nature which just here in this place have managed to assemble and erode rock masses in a way that makes you wonder if there is a greater scheme after all, a creator of the world? Perhaps that's why monasteries have been built on some of these pinnacles? We can see them from the balcony of the room we've found in Metéora; Tavern Koka Roka, the guest house at the foot of the highest peak, right by the path that goes straight up; the monastery sits on the summit as a testament to the way man can quietly adapt to a divine order, without trying to challenge or improve creation, conforming to and settling within it, according to natural laws; an eyrie, a bolt-hole, it's as if the monastery is part of the mountain, as if it's always been there, watching over the valley and those of us who struggle with mundane things.

We need something to eat. We need something to drink. The guest house is run by mother Zannetos and her alcoholic son, a fine-looking young man with red hair and a ruddy face whose veins have formed a fine blue tracery beneath his eyes, an announcement in blood presaging imminent wreck and revealing that much is ruined already. By what? Loneliness? His mother? Duty and responsibility, his dead father? An inherited weakness, alcoholism? Or is it simply that he likes drinking? He boasts about how he doesn't like travelling. He hasn't been to many places, doesn't want to go anywhere. He has no need to travel, tourists from all over the world come here, they bring their countries with them, their languages and stories; he likes to imagine what life is like in the US and Australia, Norway and Finland, but he would never contemplate going there. He's happy here, in the greatest and proudest country in the world, in the finest part of glorious Greece, right here in Metéora, at the foot of these mountains, in this house, here in the cellar with its open door that lets the sunlight in.

We sit at the table in the shade, next to the hearth where mother Zannetos is grilling pork over the embers. In the dimness of the cellar, in the light from the embers, she seems young; dark curly hair, a black blouse and long black skirt, sandals on her feet. She runs her hand through her son's hair, they could be lovers. He drinks in moderation while she's in the cellar, she's preparing food, there are five of us guests, as soon as she's finished serving, she goes up into the house, and he sits on. Arthur Zannetos waits until his mother has gone, then he gets out the homemade rosé wine that he drinks. He fetches it in earthenware pitchers, from what seems like an inexhaustible reservoir. We stay at the house for three nights and drink large quantities of the wine, he drinks even more. He doesn't bother with bottles in the bar that he runs, those foreign bottles, it's only his rosé that counts, the finest wine in all the wonder of Greece. He brags incessantly about himself and his native land. He still does all his sums in drachmas, the noblest and best currency in the whole world, before grudgingly entering the amount on his calculator to turn that august currency into euros. Arthur has nothing against the euro, it has made him richer, but what can he do with the money? He makes his own wine, sits for most of the day and all the evening and large parts of the night in the cellar drinking. There's not a lot he needs. Cigarettes, a new pair of sunglasses, perhaps a pair of leather shoes? The clothes he wears are always the same; a dark blue shirt and black trousers, brown leather shoes and no socks. He looks like a well-heeled tramp. By one in the morning he's out of cigarettes. He gives me money, sends me off to the kiosk down in the town. The trip takes me twenty minutes, when I arrive back

I can see and hear just how drunk he really is: his speech is slurred and his face looks like it's about to disintegrate, it's swollen and his eyes have filled with water, it looks as if he's crying. He is crying. The alcohol fills him up, blows him out, now it overflows; he sweats and snuffles and spits, pees outside the door. He's no longer the proprietor and host, he's a drunk, the local sot, helpless and on his way down.

As if on some secret signal, some old understanding, his mother is at the door. In her nightdress and with loosened hair, she's been drinking too, she walks resolutely, if unsteadily, across to the table where we're sitting. She grasps her son by the hair and hauls him up, gets him on to his feet and helps him out, supporting him with a good grip round his waist and almost leading him away while she comforts him and smoothes his hair with her hand.

In the morning she's back in the cellar, in the kitchen; she serves breakfast, older now, in the early light. Quick, small movements; she's the one who keeps the house going. Occasionally, at the weekends, when there are more guests in the house, Greek families taking breaks, she is helped in the cellar by a young girl, she might be fifteen or sixteen, a small, dark creature who barely says a word, she nods and serves, clears away and wipes down in silence. The radio in the kitchen plays Greek music. The sun shines through the window. The smell of fried eggs and coffee. An elderly man sits at the table by the door, half asleep. A silvery-white beard and a black hat on his head, large, thick glasses, they must be a woman's glasses, sometimes he starts and begins turning the pages of his newspaper before nodding off again. We eat scrambled eggs and a thick white goats' cheese, and drink orange juice and strong coffee. Today we're taking the steps and path up to the monastery on the summit. A day's outing. We borrow a small pack, fill it with water bottles and cold food, and include our cameras and notebooks. Patrick, John and Nick, three backpackers from Australia, are headed for the same place, we leave before them, we'd rather walk undisturbed and by ourselves, the way we're used to; me first and Narve following. He prefers walking behind, maintaining that he thinks better like that. The person in the lead always has to keep his attention on the route; to read the terrain, not lose the path, get the direction and make decisions, where should we go? Narve thinks it's good practice for me to go first, as I'm not so used to mountain walking as he is, and he's right; route finding is an important ability and requires training. I often think about pathfinders and guides when I'm in the lead, how crucial it is to find the right way, the best route forward. To find a direction and flow to the footsteps; each wrong choice breaks the rhythm of walking, breaks it up and makes it hard work. Going back to search for the correct route is one of the worst things that can befall the walker. Going the wrong way is one of the hike's most depressing experiences; it saps the stamina and tries the temper. So, it's best to take turns at going first and last, swap the responsibility of finding the way, but Narve thinks it's necessary for me to go first to learn the art of good pathfinding. And I've become good at it. I've become good at reading maps, but even more important, at reading the landscape and finding, almost by intuition or by reason and awareness, the right way through forest and scrub, across meadow and field, river and hill, mountain and upland, through valley and pass, to find the path or track, the signs of the way we're looking for. Taking the lead has made me aware of nature. It has taught me to see. Finding the right way has taught me to read a landscape; behind that ridge, under the cloud cover, there is probably a lake or a tarn. Where the mist is lying, there'll be bog. Perhaps a wood. The sea lightens the sky. Where is the sun in the sky? An anthill to the right of the pine tree, a broken branch. A sheep track. The remains of a fire, a hunters' path. Shepherds, farmers, mountain dwellers have all found the way and trodden out the path, criss-crossing every country and region; it's worth finding the beaten path and following it. Arguably there's nothing more beautiful than a good path, a narrow and well-tramped route through the forest, across the mountain, from village to village, from farm to farm. An intricate pattern of roads; footpaths, thoroughfares, the small roads that link the small places. Sometimes these old roads have been widened to accommodate horses and carts, they've carried the mails and they've turned into main roads, been tarmacked and taken through tunnels, they've become motorways and streams of traffic, and if so, slowly and concurrently, new small ways will develop, the walker's ways, we tramp them out, slowly and patiently.

I'm walking in front and Narve behind, two walking machines now, linked in movement; a stubborn, insistent rhythm, calm, not too hard, not too fast, an even flowing tempo, that good silent tempo of a couple who are travelling far.

We walk upwards. A climb of around two and a half thousand feet. The monastery is on a plateau, right on the edge of the mountain, enclosed by a stone wall; it must have been fortified and therefore threatened, the monks were soldiers too. Today the job is done by a single man, a short squat man with long hair, a full beard and thick round glasses. A long black robe, a round chimney-pot hat on his head. He looks amusing, and this Greek Orthodox priest is a humorous man; he jokes in English and German and makes little lunges with his body and arms the whole time, as if he is trying to attack us or throw us out. Instead he suddenly proffers a small wooden box full of little cakes made with honey and dipped in powdered sugar, they're light yellow and sticky; I eat two and then the priest wants to bless me. Down on your knees, he commands. I hesitate, then kneel, he holds his right hand over my head and reads out a prayer; I feel the power and the warmth from his hand. Why me? I think; is there something he can see, an accident, a problematic destiny? He prays for me. As I get up again, I do something unexpected, I begin to shadow-box, dancing round the floor and hitting out with my arms. The priest starts laughing, comes towards me and raises his guard, hits back without wanting to land anything, it's obvious he can box. We dance round the room, striking out at thin air, ducking and weaving; he uses quick short jabs and rapid footwork, breathes through his nose and drives me back against the wall before he knocks my guard away and throws a cautious punch with the flat of his hand that touches my cheek. Knockout, he cries. I'm amazed. If it had been a real fight, I'd presumably be stretched out on the floor. I've been boxing for years. I notice that his nose has been broken. You must be a Bulgarian, he jokes, they love fighting. Then he clasps his hands and lowers his head, raises it again and makes the sign of the cross to Narve and me. Now you must go, he says.

We part company, go our separate ways down into the town. I follow a path that meanders round the high rock formations, past caves and ancient settlements—once houses and churches were built in the mountain, the dead were buried in the mountain, the mountain gave protection to both living and dead, people and animals, a world of grottoes and walkways on the mountain, of caves and rooms, an ancient tower block in the mountain. On top the small depressions where the birds perch. Storeys of large empty caverns where the people lived, and below, at the bottom of the mountain, the dens of rats and foxes, snakes and salamanders, mice and feral dogs—until the path runs down to a stream surrounded by scrub. The stream runs past a ruined mill, and below the mill are the first two houses, two massive buildings of stone, as if they who live there still prefer to inhabit caves, an inherited need to seek protection behind walls of stone and rock. On a running line strung out from one house to the other, is a large, lean dog, which hurls itself forward. It's halted in its leap by the chain, hangs in the air for an instant like a furious gargoyle, a prehistoric beast with sharp teeth and clipped wings, it falls back, turns a somersault and attacks again. I follow the motor road down to the town below, find a cafe and take a seat on the corner overlooking a small market selling vegetables and flowers. It's good to be alone. Chrysanthemums, tulips, gladioli, lilies and roses, there's good companionship in flowers. You study them. Follow the arc of colour and light in the petals' curves and lines. Shadow and darkness. You remember certain things. Various thoughts come. You order a glass of ouzo. These tall, narrow glasses of milk-white liquid. They do me good. I've got the whole afternoon to myself, I'll sit in various squares in the town and drink this spirit mixed with water. Dangerous stuff. As if you're becoming hooked on a certain taste, a certain intoxication, a certain sensitivity and melancholy. A certain loneliness. Just to find a wholly special tranquillity. A wholly special peace and happiness. You look at the flowers. They're in the shade of the parasols. Nothing more is needed; I get out my notebooks and begin to write.

Out of Greece, into Turkey

Why travel? Why not just stay at home, in your room, in your house, in the place you like better than any other, your own place. The familiar house, the requisite rooms in which we have gathered the things we need, a good bed, a desk, a whole pile of books. The windows giving on to the sea and the garden with its apple trees and holly hedge, a beautiful garden, growing wild. With good neighbours, the daily stroll to the shop and back, to get the newspapers, to chat to the shopkeeper's daughters, passing the horses that stand beneath the oaks when it rains. Finding a serenity, a stillness, a deeper sense of belonging. By doing the same every day, following your ways and routines in the house, cleaning and tidying, working in the garden, seeing the same faces, doing the same walks, repeating yourself, in order to live a good and quiet life.

Like Arthur Zannetos. He doesn't travel. He sits in the chair outside the house where he lives with his mother, static, as if asleep, as if nothing in the world could prise him away from the place where he sits resting in his sunny chair. Perhaps he has slowly, grudgingly become a part of his surroundings: the ancient, distinctive mountains, the stone-built houses and the people who inhabit them?

Perhaps he's become tied to the place and to his mother, by ties he can no longer break, that he doesn't want to escape, and instead has patiently constructed his own little ambit, his own little freedom in this small place that he's become a natural part of. Early each day he goes down into the town to buy cigarettes. In the morning he sits in the sun listening to the radio, its music and voices; he doesn't like to be disturbed. If you want to talk to Arthur, you must wait until the song is over, until the voices subside, until he switches the radio off and moves into the shade where he has a glass of his home-made wine. That first glass, he says. Ah, that first kiss, he says. That first daffodil in spring, he says, and drains his glass. He enjoys telling stories, doesn't like being interrupted or disturbed: yes, that very first love, he says. He talks to himself, we listen. He loves sitting in the shadowy corner behind the table in the cellar talking. He talks himself to distraction, far away; he's been with girls from Italy and Spain, from Romania and Russia, he knows the specialities and habits, the details and secrets of these places; what they eat for breakfast in Torino and the nightlife of Barcelona, how people dance in Brasov and Moscow, their music and meals, their vodka and songs, Russian writers, Russian girls, he's met and got to know them all here; in the cellar of the guest house in Metéora. But none of this can come anywhere near Greek food, Greek scenery, Greek music and the girls here: the way they dance and walk. Arthur Zannetos rises from his seat and walks across the floor. A metamorphosis, he changes sex, rolls his hips, opens his arms and tosses his head and hair, a glance over his shoulder; this is the way a Greek girl walks out on you, he pipes, assuming a woman's voice. Goodbye. We won't be seeing each other again. He laughs. It's amusing being jilted like that, by himself. He's alone now, single. Sits down behind the table again and fills his glass with wine from the carafe. For an instant it strikes me that he's never loved a girl. Tonight, my mother's making moussaka, he says. With a fine Greek salad and plenty of good drink. It'll be a good evening, he says waving us away, he wants to be alone with his carafe and glass.

We take the bus from Metéora to Thessaloníki, a dirty noisy town, white and polished round the edges: along the mountainside and harbour. The harbour turns into a stone-paved promenade, gleaming and white, following the sea right out to where the waves beat against the breakwater which holds its protective hand round the town. We're only going to eat and sleep here: in a room for eight, bunk beds and woollen blankets, insects and fleas, a fluorescent tube on the ceiling, the sound of electricity. We lie awake until six-thirty. The train to Istanbul leaves at seven thirty-five, we carry our fleas and flea-bites with us, those badges of honour that distinguish us as travellers of the humblest class. At the station we again meet Nick from the guest house in Metéora, we take the train together across the border; a slow process, we have to get out of the train to buy visas, and then there are all the other border-crossing rituals. We roll slowly into a dark and rain-sodden Istanbul.

In Istanbul we are immediately singled out by a small gang who want to show us the way, where to we don't know. We can't shake them off, after a while they seem threatening and Nick begins to be visibly anxious; he's carrying a small pack on his chest, a larger one on his back, he resembles a helpless, vulnerable rhinoceros as he waddles up the cobbled streets holding an open umbrella over his entire load of photographic equipment and bags. It must be his first trip abroad, he's brought everything from down under, bar the kitchen sink, carrying it along with him like an Australian donkey heading for every big city bandit and horse thief. It would have been doing him a service to relieve him of some of the useless stuff that weighs him down: a hair-dryer, a novel by Salman Rushdie, two jars of homemade jam, a collapsible camera tripod and a toilet bag that would have supplied an entire Turkish football team, male or female. He unpacks his rucksacks and bags once we've finally got him safely upstairs, to a three-bedded room in a youth hostel right by Hagia Sofia. Nick Footner is nineteen and has taken a year off university to travel round Europe alone. In other words, he's one of those types who possess a good measure of courage and foolhardiness, two of the worst characteristics you can take with you on a journey. After a few hours of sharing a room in Istanbul, we like him. After several days and nights in the city we've become extremely fond of him. We feel sorry for Nick, but he gets along well, he's the type who people help.

He sleeps in the bed between ours, wearing pyjamas and with two of his own towels, which he keeps hidden from us, folded beneath his pillow. He doesn't smoke or drink. He's scared to go out in the evenings, he sits down in reception talking to other people like himself, frightened Aussies with baseball caps and All-Blacks shirts, shorts and trainers, it's a kind of uniform, they really do look like itinerant idiots.

How on earth does he spend his days? Narve asks, after Nick has gone to sleep, we're sitting on the window frame drinking raki, smoking Turkish cigarettes. He visits museums, I say. He takes photos, and notes down what he sees in a thick notebook where he collects all the tickets and napkins, beer mats and business cards he's been given. Does he drink? No, but he collects the beer mats. Today he's been to the barber in the neighbouring house, an Englishman, who cuts tourists' hair. He's had dinner at McDonald's down near the harbour where he met an Australian girl who's going with him on the boat trip to the Bosporus Strait tomorrow, he says she's beautiful. Neither of us understands the mystery that is Nick Footner. He breathes softly and doesn't snore, it's as if all the world's innocence and purity repose in that freshly washed and well-groomed body. Is he dreaming? What does he dream about? He's dreaming about how good it will be to get home to his family in Sydney, begin his studies again and marry the girl next door, Narve says.

Walking the streets of Istanbul

To walk around Istanbul, to wander aimlessly in an unknown city, seeing everything for the first time, on a Saturday morning in March; the city has been turned grey and wet by a shower of rain, now its colours stir with the sun which is breaking through the clouds, it strikes the silver-sharp towers of the minarets, the golden-coloured cupolas above the mosques, the windows of the palaces on the Sultanahmet hill, as if the city were constructed to embrace the sun. Istanbul's streets and squares have been laid out, from the hill down to the harbour in a way that receives the sun and the light, the damp, blue light from the Sea of Marmara; it brings with it a great deal of fog and rain, and the city has sought refuge under roofs and arcades, in bazaars and passageways. Large parts of Istanbul hide beneath roofs, it's a city that lives indoors as much as out; a partially hidden system of streets and markets, squares and spaces enclosed by walls and facades, gates and doors.

Behind one of these doors, in the street called Lamartine Caddesi, close to Taksim Square, behind the Aygün Plaza Hotel, in a little office, sits Merih Günay, the author who hides behind a humdrum job, he runs a small travel agency with his sister. The time is eleven-thirty, it is exactly time for Merih's first cigarette. He's trying to give up smoking, but he can't think without cigarette smoke, he can't write without cigarettes, he says. But he has been able to put off his first cigarette until his lunch break, he waits for the next one until he gets home, and then he smokes freely at home, in the evenings, as he sits thinking at his writing desk. He's written a collection of short stories. It's about smoking cigarettes, walking the streets of Istanbul, having a job you don't like, writing prose in the evenings, the rain and the fog, and love that never comes to anything. I tell him it reminds me of Pessoa. It's about me, says Merih Günay. He's young and sententious, a beautiful, unshaven face, short, dark hair and large, brown sunglasses which he dons as soon as he leaves the office, as if he's a famous author. Orhan Pamuk lives there, he says carelessly indicating a complex of flats. The Pamuk family has lived there for generations, it's a rich family, I write better than him, Günay says of Pamuk. We have the same publisher, I put in. What? Is Pamuk translated into Norwegian? Then you must take my book to your publisher, says Merih and lights his first cigarette. We walk down the main street, Istiklal Caddesi, my new friend Merih, despite his sunglasses, is recognized several times, not by readers, but by people young and old who've bought bus, train and plane tickets when visiting relatives in Izmir and Bursa. I've got pieces in several periodicals, Merih says, mainstream and underground; I write prose and poetry, experiment with all literary forms and all genres, new literature is difficult, not easily accessible, Merih says. It's the straightforward, predictable literature that people read here, he says, and which is translated, he adds sarcastically; is it the same with you? he asks. I nod. He lays his right arm across my shoulder, as if he wants to comfort me, as if he assumes I write exactly like him, as if we're in precisely the same difficult situation, and as if we're good friends and colleagues now. I notice there are others walking in the same manner, men holding one another, an intimacy I've only observed in girls; we walk the streets with our arms round each other.

Merih shows me his regular haunt, the café where he has his own table at a fixed time; I sit here for an hour, he says, like Jean-Paul Sartre. Istanbul is like Paris in the sixties, a great experiment, this is where it's happening, we will write the new literature, shape the new philosophy. French culture was suppressed by the bourgeoisie, by lethargic post-war capitalism. Turkish culture is suppressed by Islam, but also by Turkish conservatism and national-ism. In France the final reckoning came in '68, an explosion of art and action, here the reaction will come forty years later, just wait and see, we'll be marching in the streets. But Merih Günay is no Jean-Paul Sartre yet, after an hour he has to return to his office. He really does remind me more of Fernando Pessoa, tall and thin, dressed in a long thick coat and those large sunglasses which conceal the fact that he's drunk a whole bottle of red wine. I'll write my way out of this dull job, he says. But I'm not complaining, the work doesn't demand that much of me, I rest and think, make notes and sketches, and when I get home, when I go through the door of my little first-floor flat with its view over the harbour, when I'm finally seated at my desk and get out my cigarettes, that's when I come to life, he says; I build myself up into Turkey's greatest author.

To walk the streets of Istanbul, following these narrow streets that weave in and out of buildings and houses, passageways and bazaars, over- and underground, down steps and round corners, through cramped markets and alleys. To walk over or under bridges; traffic and pavements above, restaurants and stalls below, a constricted, people-choked funnel forcing its way into the underpasses to the other side; the old city. I walk along the harbour and buy fried fish in a bun from one of the boats. Follow tram lines and cobbled curves towards Sultanahmet, halt by one of the stalls selling wine, stand at the counter watching the football match on the television screen above the vendor's head. Knitted Turkish hats. Blue, brown, red, green; I've bought a black one, I've let my beard grow and trudge about in my crumpled suit, feeling like one of Istanbul's many itinerants already, slipping unnoticed into the seething mass of the city. Disappearing in the city, into that solitude amongst the crowd, there is no better loneliness. I buy some prayer beads, count the beads in the chain as I walk, one, two, three, I'm pleased I'm beginning to resemble the people who live here. Money in my back pocket. Notebooks in a shoulder bag; I walk up past the university, sit down at a pavement cafe and smoke a hookah.

Sometimes, by copying the habits and inhabitants too carefully, you can draw attention to yourself.

The city's sharpest, most alert eyes penetrate the disguise and the studied sauntering through the city streets. You become more interesting than the city's obvious guests and tourists, you are pursued. The pursuer is a young man, he appears suddenly at my side and whispers; hashish? Whisky? A girlfriend? No thanks. A boy? No thanks. I've got everything I need, I say. You're lying, he says; there isn't a man who doesn't want something I have to offer, aren't you a man? he asks. The rhetoric of the streets. I've got everything that you can offer, I lie. So why do you walk around alone all day? So why are you here in Istanbul? he asks. Come with me, I'll show you the real Istanbul. I'll be your guide, he says.

Of course there is another Istanbul, a city beneath the city, a netherworld, a life in the shadows and darkness, but do I want to see it? It will cost me both my money and my soul; I study my pursuer's face, and he does look like a character from the underworld, a scar above his cheek, a goatee beard and ferrety eyes, some of his teeth are missing. For a moment I want to say yes to this man. The real Istanbul, that's a lie, we're lying, both he and I. What's under is no more real than what's above, and I would like to see what's under; an Istanbul of nightclubs and prostitutes, hash joints and transvestites, private clubs and baths, orgies beneath the city, subterranean parties, music and half-naked bodies below the streets and mosques. No thanks, I say. He laughs. You're stubborn, he says, are you an artist? I'll show you a place where the artists go, the famous actors, writers, film people, then I'll ring some girls I know, you can choose the one you like best, and later we'll go to a club, there'll be belly-dancing and good music, nice people, I know them, I know Istanbul, my name is Ibrahim Hani, he says holding out his hand. I shake his hand. He squeezes my hand hard, holds it a long time. We've got a deal, he says, earnestly and emphatically. You're with me, Ibrahim says, and you needn't be nervous, I won't cheat you, it won't cost a lot, almost nothing, I know people. We'll drink and smoke, talk, and you will teach me something about your country, and I will teach you something about mine, and we'll meet girls, he says.

We walk together through Istanbul. It's growing dark, the street lights come on. We haven't gone far before Ibrahim cuts off to the right, down a side street and up to a door where a bouncer wearing a knitted hat is guarding a premises behind large, lighted windows. Lamps on the tables, white-tiled walls with a blue flower pattern and a light wooden floor built as stages leading up to a long bar at the back of the locale. It's half full, small side rooms and a cellar, music emanates from down there, Turkish dance music. We find an empty table, Ibrahim orders beer, gets out his mobile phone and phones his lady friends, they'll be here soon, three of them, you must choose the best, he repeats and proffers some cigarettes which have been painted with something thin and sweetish. They taste nice, after a cigarette and a few beers I'm well away. My resistance and suspicion all gone. My caution and control all gone. My new friend Ibrahim is in high good humour and entertains our corner of the place by doing little dance steps and pirouettes, he spins round and takes his jacket off and puts it on again while he flirts with the girls on the next table. He calls me his rich, European friend, take your hat off, he says. He snatches my hat off and puts it on one of the girls, it suits her. My rich European friend likes you a lot, he says to the girl with the hat who's smoking cigarettes. But we're interrupted by the three Ibrahim girls coming in through the door, it's not hard to see they're prostitutes, over made up and wearing short skirts and high heels, they come mincing into the establishment, seat themselves at our table, silent, sceptical and sullen. I've never seen three such ugly girls gathered around a table at the same time. Coarse, rotund faces. Overweight bulging bodies. Bleached hair, red-painted mouths, dull, brown, maltreated eyes painted blue and black, as if someone's thumped them and beaten them up. They need a drink, says Ibrahim. My rich European friend is paying, and now you must choose one of the girls and make her happy, he says, peremptorily eager, as if he knows this may prove difficult. I rise and take his arm, draw him across to the bar. This is impossible, I say. Send the girls home. I can't do that, he says. I don't make up their minds for them, they decide for themselves, Turkish girls are free and liberated, like European girls. They're prostitutes, I say. Like European girls, he says scornfully, furious now, as if I've insulted him. He pulls a flick knife out of his jacket pocket, concealing it in his hand, but making clear what he'll do if I don't sit down at the table again. I sit down at the table again. Ibrahim appears with two bottles of wine, his humour has returned to normal, he jokes and laughs. I've chosen the fattest of the three, and am sitting next to her, an acrid aroma of sweat and perfume. After several glasses of wine she puts her arms around me, we're sitting at the table like a couple. I smoke another of the sweet cigarettes, drink some wine and lean my head against the bosom next to me. She caresses my hair. I kiss her neck. Ibrahim is happy, I pay for what we drink and relax, half prone as I look out across the floor at the girls going up and down the stairs to the cellar. Shall we all go down and dance? I ask. The lighting is red in the cellar, there's another bar and a small stage where a young girl is dancing. The dance floor in front of her is packed with men. She's dressed up as a belly-dancer; silver embroidered bra with pearls and glass hanging from threads which become flashing spheres as they spin round in the strong stage lighting. A short silver skirt, black panties, she dances down from the stage and round the room, bank notes are thrust into the waistband of her skirt and into her bra; she stands before the men and shakes her torso, stretches back, beats the floor with her hair. It's more of a strip show than a belly-dance, and when at length she's collected enough money, she tears off her bra as well, and dances in front of the customers in the bar. She dances, her breasts dance, two hard pointed spheres which leap up and down, as if she's riding away on some invisible rhythmic broomstick that's throbbing and thumping. The music. It whips us up. I'm holding the woman who calls herself Sandra, I whisper to her. Let's go, I whisper. She nods, makes a sign to Ibrahim. We're off, I say to Ibrahim as I clasp Sandra, I'm holding on to her. He nods. But first you must pay, he says. Give me half the money now, and the rest afterwards, I'll come to the flat when you've finished, when Sandra phones, then we'll have a special party, the girls and us two, he says. Confidingly. I nod. Give him the money. Then we go up the stairs, I've got my arm round Sandra, don't release her until we're upstairs, the place is full; I let go and walk as fast as I can between the tables, out of the door and turn to the left in the dark, narrow street. Then I start running, as fast as I can.

The Lycian way

We buy bus tickets from Merih Günay. The night bus from Istanbul to Antalya. Two seats at the back of the bus, a powerful yellow Mercedes, we swish off into the night. I love such night journeys, the silence and darkness, the tiredness which surrenders to the engine that's taking us to our destination while we sit quietly and doze. The dream and the wheel, the dream and the engine; we lie still and are taken to places we don't know. Nothing is more like a dream than travelling by bus in a strange country at night. The bus halts, I wake up and get off in one of those weird, nondescript places where those who are awake leave the bus to smoke, or walk half-naked and aimless around a large deserted square illuminated by street lights. Can we still be numbered among the living? Aren't we half dead already, in an in-between zone, a no-man's-land, on our way to an unknown destination? The only security we have is the waiting bus. We are part of the bus, return to our seats and the journey continues, we drive off in the dark.

The large man next to me sleeps with his head on my shoulder. He wakes up suddenly and offers me biscuits and some coffee which he's brought in a Thermos. His words are Turkish and I answer in Norwegian, it makes no difference, there's no distance between us. Narve sits with his head against the bus window, looking out, dreaming but not sleeping. He finds it hard to sleep in strange places, sleeps little, a wakefulness that's part of the journey perhaps, maybe he only sleeps fitfully and occasionally at home too, in his own bed; I realize that I hardly ever see him asleep, as if sleep is one of his secrets, something he hides and cherishes. We drive into Antalya in the morning, change immediately into a smaller bus, a dolmuş. An old twelve-seater Fiat that fills up along the way, until there are more than twenty passengers squashed into it. After an hour's drive along the coast, a narrow, winding road that heads due south to Kaş, the bus turns off to the right and begins its climb into the mountains. We get off at Göynük, a small village at the foot of the Beydaglari Mountains . This is where the second and longer part of our journey begins; we're walking the 'Lycian Way', as described by the British writer Kate Clow, a trip of thirty days which will take us round the southern tip of Turkey, across the mountains, along the coast on a route that was acclaimed by a British newspaper as one of the ten most stunning walks in the world.

We hesitate. We wait, try to put off the actual start, the first steps towards the mountains that lie before us; high, snow-capped, beautiful. We go to a nearby cafe, have breakfast and study the maps. They aren't good, almost unusable for walkers of paths and mountain passes like us. The detailed maps are held by the army, and it's illegal to distribute them, we are thrown back on assumptions and trial and error. We must find the start, spend several hours walking round the village looking for the right take-off point for the route and the mountains. We talk to the locals and ask the way, ask about conditions in the mountains; it's as if we don't want to leave Göynük, we get caught up in the village streets and shops; shouldn't we buy some new shirts, isn't it time to get a haircut, wouldn't it be a good idea to share a bottle of wine, calm the nerves and stoke up the boilers with white wine and a few glasses of raki? We drink and smoke. Go to several small cafes and restaurants. Is this a good beginning? Reluctantly we walk out of Göynük, following a slender gravel road that runs by the bank of the river and looks as if it disappears in a cleft in the mountains. Are we ready to start? At a bend in the road, just as we can see the village slipping away behind us, we catch sight of a restaurant, a venue for outings, in the shade between the trees, small tables on a terrace beneath a roof of leaves. A good place. It's impossible to pass it by. Haven't we already got started? We're on our way, this is the start, we're not in any hurry. We sit down at one of the tables, order wine and a piyaz of haricot beans and tomatoes in sesame sauce. We tell the proprietor, Ali, that we're headed for the mountains, he fetches a map and unrolls it. It's a classified map, a military map, he lets us look at it for a few minutes and then rolls it up again, without a word. A gesture, a gift; we've discovered the way. Ali rolls up the map, ties a piece of string round it and walks in silence out to the kitchen where he makes us some packed food from bread and cheese. Have a good journey, he says. But we don't want to go. Not yet. We order another bottle of wine, discuss the map and make our calculations. A short first leg. A good beginning. We finish the wine, shoulder our packs and lurch off, up the steep gradient towards the mountains.

We've drunk too much. We have to cross the river and take off our boots. The water is freezing. The sun scorches down. The packs are too heavy, we're sweating and labouring, following a mule track over the first foothills. The landscape levels out, a plain, two tumbledown houses, one with a wooden veranda; a tremendous view over the valley and the village below. We look at each other, no words are necessary, we walk to the house and check if it's empty. It is empty. The door is broken, the windows smashed, earth and rubbish on the floor of the living room, a smell of cooking fires and alcohol, a home for down and outs. We move in. Or rather, we decide to sleep outside on the veranda. We clear a space, gather wood for a fire, lie down on our sleeping bags in the shade of the veranda. Narve's got a bottle of whisky in his pack, we open it, lie on the veranda, talking and drinking. What do we talk about? We're frightened, frightened that people may come, frightened of being attacked and robbed. We hear the calls to prayer from the mosque, dogs barking, insects, the wind in the trees and sounds from the village. The sun sinks, we're lying in the dark. It's our first night outside, under an open sky, in Turkey. We're anxious, scared. A fear that grows and becomes more infectious with the darkness and the sounds from the village; they seem closer, they seem threatening, it begins to get cold. We light the fire, put on sweaters and woolly hats, get into our sleeping bags, two jittery vagrants. We drink whisky and feel how the alcohol anaesthetizes our fear, how the fear evaporates with every swig we take from our plastic cups, and after half a bottle of whisky the fear is gone. Our mood starts to improve, we talk more loudly and less cautiously, we shout and laugh. We are the itinerants, Narve says pulling his knife out from his sleeping bag, holding it up in the light of the fire, as if he's suddenly transformed by that thought; we're the dangerous ones, he says. It's people like us we're frightened of, he laughs and stands up on the veranda, waves his knife, as if wanting to banish whatever there is of evil intent and evil thoughts; we are the vagrants, it's us you should be frightened of, he says to our two doppelgangers, who lie sleeping on the veranda.

We spend the whole night rolling back and forth in our sleeping bags. A cold and beautiful night. We fall asleep and wake fitfully, right through until dawn. A cock crows, there are calls to prayer from the mosque and light arrives with the sun, bringing warmth. We pull our hats over our eyes, sleep for a few hours in the sun and the warmth. We sleep until it's too hot to lie in our bags wearing hats and sweaters, jackets and trousers; we get up, eat our packed food and drink lots of water, on with our boots and packs, we're ready to go.

A stiff climb, we walk through a pine forest. The intoxicating smell of pine needles and earth, the sun is striking through the branches and defrosting grass and leaves, there's a crunching as we walk. We sweat away the tiredness and the cold, sweat away the alcohol and the fears, worries and words, we walk ourselves warm. A few hours ago it was too cold, now it's too hot, our packs are too heavy, but we can't jettison any of our clothes, we throw away washing things and books, we throw away all the little things that weigh too much, a sandwich box, a thermo jug, deodorants and novels, Thomas Mann and Virginia Woolf. We dump everything that isn't vital, until we have the perfect weight of just what we need; around twenty-five pounds of food and clothing, drink and sleeping bags. No insulating mats, no tents or additional equipment, we'll be walking hard and far.

When boots are good, when the pack isn't too heavy and lies unnoticed on the back, when clothes are dry and not yet saturated with sweat or rain, it's great to walk. There is nothing better than walking; moving along unaided, putting one foot in front of the other and gliding into a kind of oblivion which is at the same time a heightened presence; we forget we're walking, we forget the act of walking and the effort of moving, while simultaneously seeing and hearing more acutely, smelling more keenly, we experience it all more powerfully: a bird flies up. The sunlight strikes the tree crowns, the earth steams. A small clump of white anemones, shining. Water that flows, still water. A stream with trout resting behind stones in a pool, we drink the water. Snow that's melting, tracks in the snow. A carpet of bog, cotton grass swaying in the wind. We think less when we're walking far, we slip into a walking rhythm and thoughts cease, become a concentrated attention that is turned on all we see and hear, all we smell; this flower, this breeze, these trees, as if thoughts mutate to become part of what they encounter; a river, a mountain, a road.

It doesn't take long before boots are rubbing, before clothes are soaked with sweat and the only thing we're thinking about is where to get some relief from the sun. A hard climb, burning heat, heavy clothes, the weight of the packs, aching muscles, hammering hearts, gasping breath, legs moving but not of their own accord now, we push them, force them on. We have a rule, an agreement about not complaining, that we never moan to each other; a single expression of displeasure when the going is tough would be enough to ruin the rest of the day's walk for both of us. Grumbling can ruin an entire trip, as we know, we walk in silence. It is this silence that enables us to get along so well together, to do long hard journeys, to stay together, with hardly any space; with no space other than our own thoughts and the hundred yards that separate us as we walk; we walk singly, each in his own silence.

Narve falls, has he broken a rib? He doesn't say a word. I go through some brush, tear my skin to shreds, bleed from my arm and stomach. We laugh at this when we arrive at the point where we've decided to halt, our resting place. We lie in the grass and laugh at our injuries, at our dogged silence, we laugh at the mosquito and insect bites, at the blisters and bruises. We laugh at our new aspect, a swollen eye, chapped lips and sunburnt skin; we look like two hobos, torn jackets and trousers with mud and dirt to the knees. We lie in the grass and laugh at what we look like. And this is just the start, Narve says; I wonder what we'll look like after a week, or when we arrive, when we saunter into Fethiye to order piyaz and red wine at a restaurant.

Perhaps we won't arrive, I say.

What do you mean?

That it might be difficult to go back, to normality, to what was before, before we started walking, I don't know, but it could be that this really is a beginning, the beginning of something new, a totally different life, a different lifestyle.

Hours in the grass, hours in the shade. Before we climb steeply to reach Göynÿk Yaylasi which means High Göynük. On the hilltop there is another ramshackle house, it's on high stout stilts, a staircase leading up to it; we break open the door and the living room is empty, apart from some old blankets thrown on the floor. We decide to spend the night here, wipe the floors with the blankets and then hear the sound of a whistle. We go out on to the steps, and behind the house, under an orange tree, is a man with a white beard and black hat, with a whistle in his mouth. He blows his whistle and raises his arm above his head, straight up in the air, and lets it fall to his thigh, it's the herdsman's sign to his dog to come here, but he has no dog, the sign is for us. He repeats the movement: come here. We look at one another, Narve and I. It's an invitation, I say. The goatherd stands under his tree surrounded by goats, he blows his whistle and yet again makes the sign with his arm. Come here. We obey and walk towards the goatherd, who lifts his other hand to his mouth which he opens and closes and makes chewing movements with his teeth; it's an invitation to eat, I say. We fetch our packs and follow him, he walks along the wooded ridge followed by his goats and two hungry hikers; we walk along the ridge and watch the house gradually emerging from the tree around which it has been built, like those tree-houses we built as children, apart from the fact that this house has solid walls two storeys high climbing up the tree trunk whose lowest branches are growing into the roof which is pitched and overgrown with flowers and grass. A beautiful house. A simple house with a small veranda and an extension on the back: the kitchen and running water that is pumped from the well by an old tractor engine. We clamber up the steps, remove our boots and are shown into a small living room where an elderly woman is sitting on the floor swathed in a heavy coat and a kerchief, she's got a beard like a man's, but the face of a woman, a round, ruddy face contorted with pain, her eyes are pressed shut, and she makes little whimpering sounds as she rocks her body to and fro.

Ramazan the goatherd points to Narve and makes it clear that he wants him to examine the woman on the floor. This is all very strange, Narve is a doctor's son, and in his white shirt perhaps he does resemble a doctor; he always has a small assortment of medicines with him; painkillers, sedatives and sleeping pills, could it be that Ramazan has picked up the medical tendency in him, or is it simply a desperate hope, a hope that someone can help? Doctor Drink bends down and examines the woman on the floor. One foot is badly swollen; it's an inflammation that may be caused by her kidneys, Narve tells me; there's nothing I can do, he says, she ought to have antibiotics, I'll give her painkillers, an opiate, it's all I've got that can get us out of this situation.

After the examination and treatment, which soon appears to be successful, the old woman, who is Ramazan's wife, gets to her feet and immediately seems younger; she makes us all food. We sit on the floor of the other room in the house, a combined bed–sitting room; a pallet on which Ramazan sleeps, a mattress on the floor for his wife, and between their beds there is a stove. The stove is fed with birch wood and both temperature and spirits rise. We are served chicken soup and bread which we dip in a yoghurt-like cream, Followed by soft-boiled eggs with pepper and that marvellous bread which has been heated on the stove. We drink ice-cold water. Then we watch the news on a small television set and drink Turkish tea with some sweet round cakes. It's cigarette time. We walk out on to the small veranda, there is a full moon. Ramazan's eyes have tears in them. He is happy, it seems. Narve is worried, he's wondering if he oughtn't to give Ramazan our stock of painkillers; she needs a doctor, he tells Ramazan. Ramazan nods and pats Narve on the shoulder; doctor, he exults, appreciative and happy.

We sleep in an outhouse, a small shack with an iron bed which is just big enough for two if we lie in opposite directions. A paraffin lamp, two pillows and some blankets among which Ramazan has hidden packets of cigarettes and bottles of spirits; this is his den, we sleep long and well. We're woken up by Ramazan standing in the doorway, he makes the sign with his hand and his mouth; it's breakfast. We sit on the floor of the living room, eating eggs and bread, with coffee and water. Ramazan's wife is asleep on her mattress, knocked out by the tablets, or perhaps simply by all the sleep that's unexpectedly come her way. Ramazan is still feeling happy, Narve is still worried, he gives Ramazan all his analgesic tablets. Then he digs out a packet of American cigarettes and some Turkish money, but Ramazan won't take the money. The money is for a doctor, Narve says and Ramazan nods and embraces him; doctor, Ramazan repeats and lights a cigarette.

We make for Gedelme; a level, light journey along a valley, on a well-walked forest track, a road for goatherds and hunters. We meet a twelve-year-old girl, looking after a flock of more than twenty goats, walking with a stick in one hand and a stone in the other, tools that haven't changed in the past two thousand years. A couple of grouse fly up, and a bit later we bump into a hunter, he's carrying his gun in a sling across his shoulder. A short man with a moustache and a three-cornered hat, with a feather in it, he really does look every bit the hunter. I photograph him, he poses taking aim at the photographer; it's a frightening but totally risk-free picture. We walk at an even, relaxed tempo, Narve ahead and me a few hundred yards behind, this means it's my turn to think. What am I thinking about? The better the going, the easier it is to fall into meaningless thoughts; thoughts are lighter, I've walked off all I had of anxieties and serious ideas, I no longer think about what I'll do when the hike is over: where I'll live and what I'll write, gradually as we move forward, my thoughts go in the opposite direction, they go back, further and further back in time; I think about my youth and child-hood, meander back to where I've been before, just as we're walking towards something unknown and new.

Gedelme is nothing more than a crossroads with a few houses and a little booth which is a kitchen, in other words an eating place with three plastic tables and chairs next to a hatch from which a woman is peering. We're on our way down from the first mountain crossing, should we eat here or wait until we get right down to Çirali on the coast? Just as we're about to sit down, a lorry draws up at the stall, the driver buys a bottle of Coke, we ask him if we can cadge a lift down to the main road. He nods and we jump up on the back of the lorry which is already occupied by an elderly woman sitting on a stool. Three goats are tethered to the back of the cab, a young boy is looking after them, his father is guarding a cock which has its feet tied, it is anxious and knows where it's going; to the slaughter. The family drinks tea from a Thermos, it would look like a family outing, were it not for the goats and the cock which is in frantic revolt, it doesn't want to die. Each time the man stands up or releases his grip on the bird, it tries to twist round to get to its feet, it topples, falls, is overpowered and held fast. One pupil expands and contracts in its eye, as if its escape continues inside the cock; we sit rigid with compassion and alarm at this struggle with mortality, become complicit in this fearful journey of death towards the cock's extinction. It cries out. Narve blocks his ears, I shield my eyes, we don't say a word, sit silent on the back of the lorry waiting impatiently for the journey to be over. It's as if the cock's journey is the opposite of our own; we're travelling to a beginning, it's travelling towards an end. Or perhaps the cock's way to death brings back our own fears; every beginning must have an end. We sit on the lorry and are shaken by the cock's fight for life; both of us are excessively afraid of dying.

A sojourn at Olympos

This exaggerated fear of death, where does it come from? Is this the end? The end of our journey, does it end here? We jump off the lorry, jog down the road, away from death and the cock; it haunts us for the rest of the trip, as a new kind of silence, a revived dread. We walk along the main road, the cars flash past, this sudden speed, this murderous haste, these dark invisible faces that fly past; we teeter on the edge of the road, articulated lorries, buses, vans, private cars, tractors and no pedestrians, apart from us; two tiny figures on the highway, a step too far to the left and it's curtains, over, finished, the journey's at an end, it ends here, but we keep our balance, we walk the tightrope and do not fall, either to the left or to the right, we walk straight ahead, one foot in front of the other, on the yellow road-marking towards Çirali.

We enter the small seaside village in the evening, it's dark. We've walked on the highway in the dark, on asphalt, our feet are swollen, the blisters hurt like wounds, our shoulders ache, our backs ache, our heads ache; how forlorn the pedestrian is, how terribly helpless he is, in the dark, on the road, so small, so insignificant on the road, in the dark; road and sky, they merge in a great, dark nothingness. Why are we walking here, where to? Why aren't we sleeping in a bed, in a house, a home, in the same room together; isn't it true that we wake and sleep simultaneously? To love? Love requires that we be at rest, that we settle down, that we remain in the same place; motion is loneliness.

We walk along the beach, searching for a place to sleep. The lights from the houses, residences, homes, a guest house, two vacant beds in a room, we go in. We've found a good place to sleep. Take our clothes off, lie on the beds and smoke, share a half bottle of raki which we mix with water. That pleasant buzz. How nice it is to lie in bed smoking. We can hear sounds from the bar outside the window, music, Lou Reed, laughter and clinking glass; how good it is to lie in bed and hear the voices of young girls drinking.

In the morning we set off with our packs along the beach. Towards Olympos. White sand, stretching away, clear, blue sea and waves washing over feet that need rest, we need rest, we must rest now. We decide to spend a few days on the beach. We walk up through the temple ruins, follow a river, and just where the river curves, on some open ground, behind a gate overgrown with white hawthorn, we find the perfect spot. A camp, a barracks, and behind the barracks little cabins among the trees.

We rent a cabin each, there are chinks between the planks of the thin walls, a mattress on the floor, a woollen blanket, that's all. It's enough, the cabin is good and simple, the sunlight filters through the cracks of the walls and gives the small room a touch of warmth. From the huts some narrow steps lead down to a small path laid with flagstones, like little streets between the houses in the trees, they all lead to the barracks where there is a large open room with a woodstove in the middle. Long wooden tables arranged around the stove, sawdust on the floor, a kitchen behind the curtain that hides the cooks, two Polish students. They dish up three meals a day, breakfast, lunch and supper, in the evening they open a bar in the corner of the room, for those of us who want to stay up at night; the barracks is a focal point for everyone who lives in the cabins, tourists, hippies, students and a large gaggle of unidentified souls who stay here for shorter or longer periods. As we quickly discover, the camp is a difficult place to leave. During the days we lie on the beach, rest and swim, take short walks in the hills around the camp, and after lunch we lie in our cabins reading. When darkness falls and it turns cold, we walk the short distance to the barracks where we eat and sit round the stove talking and listening to music, drinking raki and smoking cigarettes. A good life. A simple life in a small community inside the big one, outside the normal rules and systems; we form our own habits and pander to our own inclinations, we sleep late, eat well and drink a good deal as we sit up discussing philosophy and literature; Germans, Poles, Americans, Turks and two Norwegians who can't tear themselves away, and have taken up residence amongst the trees to do what they like best; reading and idling away the time.

One evening a family is occupying one of the tables in the barracks. The father is in his fifties and looks good dressed in his pressed beige flannel trousers and white short-sleeved shirt. His wife is beautiful, she is younger than him, his daughters are lovely, they attract attention. Who are they? What is this family doing here? I'm sitting drinking with Andreas as usual, he suffers from tinnitus, a constant noise in his head, it made him almost mad, ruined his marriage and forced him to give up his job, one day he went, left Berlin and his house and friends; if not I'd have committed suicide, he says soberly, a statement of fact, Andreas is taciturn and difficult, he keeps himself to himself, has a powerful aura of loneliness and gravity. The others avoid him and we sit on our own, I enjoy listening to a man who the others claim hasn't spoken a coherent sentence since he's been here; we talk about love. We talk about all the difficult things, all the good things, we talk about everything imaginable. Andreas has thick, long dark hair and a substantial beard, his face is in the process of vanishing behind all the hair, his glasses have thick lenses, but his eyes shine when he talks and a wide sensual mouth gives him away, he's a handsome man. We sit watching the newly arrived family, they eat, and after the meal the father sits drinking alone, he's drinking raki. Suddenly he starts singing, a Beatles song, he sings 'Dear Prudence' and afterwards 'Blackbird', and when at last he commences on 'Rocky Raccoon' I can't resist, I sing along. We sing most of *The White Album*, but then the father is interrupted by his wife and daughters who have showered and changed and titivated themselves, they think it's embarrassing that an elderly man should be sitting with all these youngsters singing. They shush him and smack his mouth fondly, but the father beckons us over to his table and we sing 'Ob-La-Di, Ob-La-Da' and 'While My Guitar Gently Weeps'. We drink raki and the father tells us that he's a colonel in the Turkish Army and that he was a hippie when he was young and that he wants to show his wife and daughters what his former life was like. I was a proper hippie, with long hair and a beard, rather like him, he says pointing to Andreas, and now I'm an army colonel, it's not as different as perhaps you think. I'm still the same person.

The colonel drinks raki and gets drunk, his wife and daughters try to steer him towards bed, they pull him and push him, but he just sits on. I love my wife, he says embracing and kissing her; and I love my daughters, he says, and everyone in the barracks can see they're a happy family. Andreas has tears in his eyes, he turns away and wipes his glasses on his shirt, this family scene reminds him of something, and it reminds me of something too; I put an arm around Andreas, and there we sit, like two accessories to a crime without name.

Finally his young wife manages to wheedle the colonel to bed, she follows him out of the barracks and over to the cabin, but quickly returns and sits down with her daughters who are entertaining Andreas and me with stories about their father, he's an amusing man, a good father, a companion and friend. For the first time I hear Andreas talk to people other than me, he speaks long and earnestly to the two daughters. I sit spellbound. I've never heard anyone talk so wisely and well as Andreas does to the girls. The daughters and their mother sit silently listening, just as I do, we can't tear ourselves away from each other that magic night, we sit up around the stove until morning comes. How will the party break up? None of us wants to get up and go to bed, none of us wants to call time, we don't want to sleep. A wakeful night. One of the finest nights I've ever experienced; the three women and Andreas who talks like a father.

I sleep for three hours and am woken by Narve who wants to leave, he's restless and wants to get going, out on the road again, up into the mountains, down to the rest of the coast and along the planned route. But I must say goodbye to Andreas and the family, I say. I don't want to leave, not yet, there are things still unfinished, that I don't want to finish so abruptly, I think and raise objections; can't we stay a few days more? There is something that ties me to Andreas, and to the colonel and his wife and two daughters, something indiscernible and important, I think as I dress unwillingly, strap on my pack, hungover and sleepy, follow Narve across to the barracks where we have breakfast and settle up, before leaving, without a single word of farewell to my new family.

Homesickness

It's getting near the end of April, May is approaching. We turn up from the camp at Olympos, cross the river and walk through a tunnel of woods, past the ruins of a small town on the high ground with a view over the sea. A dead dog is lying in the middle of the path. It's light grey, but with a dirt-darkened belly, perhaps it has dragged itself along, crawled and struggled before it had to give up and lay down to die.

A sudden end to the path ahead, on a perfectly ordinary day. The dog is stiff and its eyes are open, there is no wound or rent in its coat, it lies uninjured on the path untouched by birds and other animals. We leave it there and proceed up a goat track. There are donkey roads and mule tracks and sheep paths; animals give their names to the routes in the mountains; we take the narrow path out towards the sea, towards Cape Gelidonia and the lighthouse we've seen marked on the map.

The lighthouse is unmanned but outside the old lighthouse keeper's dwelling is a spring, we drink from it and rest. The walk from the lighthouse down to the beach at Karaoz is one of the highlights of the trip; a lovely stretch through pine woods and across open plains where horses stand beneath huge oaks. Sheep grazing, donkeys, goats, all roaming free, a foretaste of the farms lying below at the foot of the mountains. We pass small steadings and summer farms, and from this altitude we can see the vast tomato plantations; the greenhouses twinkle like snow on the flat, serrated landscape; a plain partitioned out in plastic and glass. When we get closer, the greenhouses turn transparent; we can see the blood-red tomatoes, the way they swell and press against the sides and roofs in the hothouses which threaten to burst, and are cracked and punctured by the growing plants. Narrow walkways run between the green-houses, children play, dogs, cats, hens, rats, and at the end of the labyrinth there's a terrace with a canvas awning, and a couple of feet above the ground, in a chair sheltered by the awning, sits a large fat man in a black cap, smoking a cigar.

He looks like some petty king, and presumably that's what he is, he beckons us to him and we're invited to sit with him in the shade of the terrace. I've taken a tumble in the mountains and am bleeding from my chest and one leg, the large man on his throne puts his fingers in his mouth and whistles. He shouts and gives orders and soon both mother and daughter emerge from the house to wash and tend my wounds. They boil water, cut up a cloth and wash the injuries before putting on an ointment that stings and burns, that's a good sign. The daughter is young, she blushes and looks down as she smoothes the ointment over my skin; I get embarrassed and look up. Raise my eyes as much as I can to avoid looking at the young body and the young hands that are working just below my chest. I put on a clean shirt, and now three bowls of hot soup are brought out; lentils and peas in oil and yoghurt, it tastes bitter but needs to be flavoured with cinnamon and sugar, and that makes the meal perfect; we eat as the tomato king talks in Turkish and Russian. We are offered raki and water, and now the language barrier no longer presents any difficulty, we listen and nod, drink and smoke, we reply in Norwegian and the conversation proceeds of its own accord, in its own special direction, we point at the sea. We are heading for the beach, we will rest and sleep on the beach.

On the beach at Karaoz there's a bungalow that contains a bar with a small TV screen; it's showing the Premier League match between Real Madrid and Bayern Munich. We watch the match and soon decide we're rooting for the Germans. The Spanish home supporters hurl lighters and coins at Michael Ballack and Oliver Kahn, the German team is struggling, against football technique and loutish supporters, and wins the game by one goal. We sit in the bar eating nuts and drinking beer, as if we haven't moved a single foot from the journey's start, as if all the exertion and distance is wiped away by a few minutes of football and beer. How many times, in how many places have we sat just like this in a bar and roared at players running across a pitch in Madrid or London, Manchester or Milan? We've come home. But it only lasts a few hours, once the match is finished and we've gone over the details, when we've got drunk on raki and beer and must leave the bar to find somewhere to sleep, we're suddenly back abroad; on a lonely and deserted beach in Turkey, in the off-season, in the darkness beneath the stars and a cold open sky.

We each find our own bed on the beach, wrap up in all our thick clothes and creep into our sleeping bags, and for the first time during our hike I get a severe bout of homesickness.

Homesickness. It's an inevitable part of all journeys, we're exhausted and wish for home; the homesickness grows, strengthens and permeates every part of the body; the feet want home, the hands, the heart, the thoughts want home. We've had enough, seen enough, heard enough, experienced more than we can bear, and the homesickness spreads through our bodies like a lazy indifference, a lethargy that can no longer be bothered to relate to further moves and changes, meetings and places. The journey back has already begun, we think of home and are going home in our thoughts, even though we've still got a long journey ahead, we haven't reached the halfway mark, but it's as if the road has made a subtle turn, it's rounded a bend and after that bend the direction is different; it's trending slowly and imperceptibly back. The homeward journey can't be pin-pointed on the map, it begins in the body and moves to the head and is transmitted to the feet; now we're walking home. We turn into a species of somnambulists, we plod on half asleep, half speed ahead, sauntering along with half the will, less energy and a strong desire for rest; to come home and sleep in a good and familiar bed. Homesickness comes suddenly, but it vanishes quickly too, it's a bit like going up a steep hill, we begin to tire and want to give up, want to go down again and return to the bed we left, but—with a pure effort of will—we continue the ascent, reach the top and rest with a tremendous view of the place into which we'll descend; a new and alluring place.

We're approaching the town where we're to rest, a week by the sea, on the beach at Kaş. It's roughly half way along the route, we plan to walk round the point of the coast all the way to Fethiye where we'll take the bus back to Istanbul. From there we'll take the night train to Bucharest, and the train from the Romanian capital to Braşov and Sighişoara where we'll dispense with all modern methods of transport and continue on foot, across the mountains of Transylvania.

How does a journey end? We arrive, is that a new beginning or an ending? How far can we walk, how long will we stick to the road; we're both getting really tired, our boots have holes in them and the soles are worn, our clothes are ripped and ruined, we're covered in blisters and injuries, sprains and cuts, is this the start of something decisive and different, a life as tramps and wayfarers, or is it the end of a long walking trip through parts of Greece and Turkey?

We can choose. We've got plenty of time, we have the whole of the summer and autumn before us, there's no hurry, we can stay at the beach for a few weeks and rest, stay at a good hotel, buy new clothes and boots, we've got enough money, nothing is stopping us, no jobs or commitments, nothing apart from bad consciences and homesickness, we're footloose and free.

We grew up in the same place, in the same street, and we never knew each other, went out separate ways, although we took the same route, the road to school, or the path through the forest to the football pitch; we never met, not until I moved to Sunnfjord with my new family, and there, in the library at Førde, I bumped into Narve one day while he was reading one of William Dalrymple's books: *A Journey in the Shadow of Byzantium*. It was the start of a friendship that would revolve around books and travel. It was the beginning of a journey that still isn't complete, it shuttles back and forth in time and space, the further we get from the place we both call home, the closer we get to the time when we didn't know each other, all the years we spent in the same streets, in the same houses and buildings, in the same places, doing our separate things, of course. There are many ways to travel, and there are many ways of being at home; we travel backwards and forwards in time and geography, in books and stories, short and long journeys of the imagination and the memory, on maps and in unknown regions; we can sail away in our own sitting rooms. We can sit down in any old chair in front of the desk by the window and start writing.

This journey ends here.

We get there, arrive at our planned resting place by the sea. We look down at the town from above, it climbs up the mountainside and down again towards the sea which comes silently into the small bays with their beaches and rocks. We will swim and recuperate, sleep and read, make notes and write. At Kaş we live separately, spend our days alone and walk about its streets without bumping into one another, follow our own habits and patterns, as we did before we knew each other; we walk round the same town like two strangers, until one day we may chance upon each other in a street or in cafe. Then one of us will raise his eyes from the book he's reading and give the other a look of restless expectation: are you ready? Are you ready to hoist your pack and set out on the open road?

Epilogue

Why not end with a road; the road I walk along every single day from the house where I live down to the shop by the sea, it's my favourite road, the road I like walking best of all. It begins at my desk and goes out of the door into a little hall which divides into two parts; I can go up the stairs to the bedrooms, or I can go out of the front door, which brings me on to a small covered landing with stairs leading down to the gravel path that goes through the garden, past the apple trees and the holly, out of the gate towards the narrow, asphalt side road; I can turn to the left or to the right.

Each day I turn to the left (to the right only if I'm picking up the post or trundling the wheelie bin to the turning place by Kongshaugen which has a marvellous view of the sea, right across to the small pinpoints of city lights in the far distance, or it might be that the city isn't there, vanished behind mist and cloud, it's not uncommon, the city is more often invisible than not; I don't miss it) and follow the side road past a broken-paned greenhouse and down a steep hill, veering to the right as it passes my neighbour's house and an old barn which is overgrown with avens; the hedge is unnaturally green and full of bees that buzz with an electric hum, it's like walking past something natural that isn't part of nature, it's the same with the greenhouses, they're punctured by vines, and orange trees push out through the broken panes. The gravel road makes a turn, and just here the landscape opens up on both sides; a meadow of wild flowers and grass, which grows in waves right down to the sea. The path takes off to the right, through a wood, you cross an electric fence and suddenly find yourself in a clearing, you have to stop; I am brought to a halt by the sudden, soft light and the stillness which is more marked here than at other points along the route. A clearing, it surprises me every time, perhaps because of the absence or the emptiness that strikes you in such a place; there's nothing here but moss and heather, bilberry bushes and fallen leaves. The path is soft, it follows the tracks of horses, they churn up the ground, an expanse of mud, this is the enclosure itself, and here are the horses, each usually standing under its own tree, it's raining. A mild, transparent rain, imperceptible, almost. I walk past the stalls and two houses, the marina and boat sheds standing in a semicircle around it, wooden boats and plastic boats, motorboats and sailing boats. The path joins a metalled side road; I walk through a residential estate with gardens and raspberry canes, white wooden buildings and garages, cars and machinery, the usual clutter outside the houses, we live ordinary lives. The road crests a hilltop and turns down past the jetty after which it carries on up to the shop.

The shop is run by a couple and their two daughters. You open the door and walk right into a kind of home. The family members have found their fixed places around the premises, behind the meat counter and in the store room, on the till and in the rest room out through the back where you can eat and have coffee, smoke and use a phone. The shop isn't large, but it contains all you need. You don't really need all that much. I buy a newspaper and a some cigarettes, walk quickly back to the house and sit down to write.

I'm writing a book about walking. For a long time now I've been sedentary, I've been no further than this daily walk to and from the shop. Maybe I'll take the bus into town; maybe I'll go on a longer walk; I'll go through my gate and turn to the right and set off for the only peak on the island, it's barely more than a thousand feet high, but it's enough to give me a kind of panorama, of the island and the house I'm living in; seen from the summit it doesn't look all that different from all the other houses on the island.